Silas K. Hocking

Rex Raynor

A Story of Sowing and reaping

Silas K. Hocking

Rex Raynor
A Story of Sowing and reaping

ISBN/EAN: 9783337284862

Printed in Europe, USA, Canada, Australia, Japan

Cover: Foto ©Andreas Hilbeck / pixelio.de

More available books at **www.hansebooks.com**

LIST OF WORKS

BY

SILAS K. HOCKING.

In large crown 8vo., Cloth Gilt, fully Illustrated, Price 3s. 6d. each.

ONE IN CHARITY.
A SON OF REUBEN.
THE HEART OF MAN.
CALEB CARTHEW.
FOR ABIGAIL : A West Country Story.
WHERE DUTY LIES.
FOR LIGHT AND LIBERTY.
FOR SUCH IS LIFE.
IN SPITE OF FATE.
GOD'S OUTCAST.
THE DAY OF RECOMPENSE.
THE STRANGE ADVENTURES OF ISRAEL PENDRAY.
TO PAY THE PRICE.
THE FATE OF ENDILLOE.
GRIPPED.
THE WIZARD'S LIGHT.
A BONNIE SAXON.
THE TEMPTER'S POWER.
THE SCARLET CLUE.
THE FLAMING SWORD.
THE SQUIRE'S DAUGHTER.
PIONEERS.
THE SILENT MAN.
A MODERN PHARISEE.
THE SHADOW BETWEEN.
YOURS AND MINE.

In Crown 8vo., Cloth Gilt, Gilt Edges, fully Illustrated, Price 2s. 6d. each,
or ditto   ditto   Plain Edges   ditto   Price 2s. 0d. ,,

HER BENNY: A Story of Street Life.
IVY: A Tale of Cottage Life.
HIS FATHER ; or, A Mother's Legacy.
ALEC GREEN : A Tale of Sea Life.
SEA WAIF: A Tale of the Sea.
DICK'S FAIRY: A Tale of the Streets
CRICKET: A Tale of Humble Life.
REAL GRIT.
CROOKLEIGH: A Village Story.
TREGEAGLE'S HEAD : A Romance of the Cornish Cliffs.
REEDYFORD ; or, Creed and Character.
CHIPS, JOE AND MIKE.
REX RAYNOR, ARTIST.
DOCTOR DICK.
THE BLINDNESS OF MADGE TYNDALL.
WHEN LIFE IS YOUNG.
THE CONQUERING WILL.

A Special Illustrated Edition, in medium 8vo., Cloth Gilt, Price 3s. 6d.

HER BENNY: A Story of Street Life.   Illustrated with 47 original
Engravings.

LONDON: FREDERICK WARNE & CO. ; AND NEW YORK.

REX RAYNOR, ARTIST.

REX RAYNOR, ARTIST

A STORY OF SOWING AND REAPING

BY

SILAS K. HOCKING

AUTHOR OF

"HER BENNY," "FOR ABIGAIL," "REAL GRIT,"
ETC.

WITH ILLUSTRATIONS BY HAROLD COPPING

LONDON
FREDERICK WARNE AND CO.
AND NEW YORK

CONTENTS.

REX RAYNOR, ARTIST.

CHAPTER I.

THE PARTING OF THE WAYS.

'Ill masters good, good seems to change
    To ill with greatest ease ;
And, worst of all, the good with good
    Is at cross purposes.'—*Faber*.

NEVER had *right* appeared so difficult before. Never had *wrong* seemed so full of promise as now. Indeed, to Jane Raynor's darkened and bewildered sense, right and wrong might have changed places, and judgment and conscience dropped out of existence altogether. She had been in trying circumstances before—many times, in fact, and oft; for with an ailing family and a small and precarious income, life had not been all a bed of roses; a bed of thorns would, perhaps, more truly describe it. Still, in the past, right had always seemed right—had always commended itself to her judgment and conscience alike; while

1

duty, however difficult, had ever lain clear and distinct before her.

Now, however, it was no longer so. At the moment our story opens she was seated in a low rocking-chair with a look of horror in her eyes. Across her knees lay a month-old baby, upon whose pure and gentle face death had unmistakably set its seal. At her feet was a cradle, in which was another babe of about the same age, apparently in perfect health and fast asleep.

The children were not twins, nor in any way related to each other. The child in the cradle was her own; that upon her knee the firstborn of Jonas Brown, Esq., J.P., and his young wife May. Poor Mrs. Brown was still lying at the point of death, and the doctors were almost despairing of her recovery. The one thing that seemed to hold her to life was the little child whom she had hardly strength to see, much less to nurse. But every day she whispered her inquiries for its welfare, and when she learned he was well and growing, she would smile sweetly and close her eyes again.

The doctors who attended her suggested that Mrs. Raynor should be asked to nurse the infant along with her own, and, for the sake of the large pay that was offered, Mrs. Raynor readily acceded to the request. And so it came about that the son and heir of the rich banker was taken to the home of the poor artist, and laid in the arms of his wife.

Jane Raynor was a good woman in the main;

a little fretful, perhaps, and given to melancholy; but that was scarcely to be wondered at. Life had gone hardly with her of late. Money had been scarce, her husband had been ill, and the children cross and unmanageable; and so the advent of her youngest born had brought no joy with it. Indeed, if the truth must be told, the little fellow was not wanted. He came where there seemed no room for him, and no means for his maintenance. John Raynor was confined to his bed at the time with an acute attack of bronchitis, brought on by sketching out of doors in the teeth of a keen east wind.

He was a brave man, patient, true, and uncomplaining. It had been a great grief to him that his pictures had not sold, and that in consequence the wolf of want seemed ever howling about the house. For himself, he did not mind so much, but it troubled his heart sorely to see his wife so worried and vexed, and to note how rapidly her good looks had faded under the stress of hard times.

He was too ill to notice the child when it was born. The old woman who acted the part of nurse carried it to his bedside; but the effort of raising himself to look at its little puckered face brought on a fit of coughing, and so he scarcely saw it.

'It's only a little 'un,' said the old woman; 'but it's in a big world; an' so there's plenty of room for it to grow in.'

'I'm most anxious about Jane,' he struggled to say.

'Oh, she's agoin' on all right,' was the cheerful answer; 'so don't you never fear, but make haste an' get well yourself.'

'I'll try,' he answered with a feeble smile; and then he found himself alone again.

Jane Raynor was up and about before her husband. 'Poor folks cannot afford to waste their time in bed,' she explained to the doctor, who had remonstrated with her. 'Besides, my old nurse had to leave me; and so there was no help for it.'

She took no harm, however; on the contrary, she gathered strength rapidly when she got downstairs, and when, a few days later, her husband crept feebly into the little sitting-room, he declared she was looking her old self again, in spite of having two babies to nurse.

He smiled at the splendid hammock-cradle, all polished brass and filigree work, which stood in a corner of the room and in which slept the banker's child. It seemed such a contrast to the well-worn wicker bassinette in which his own child lay.

'You must take care you don't get the children mixed, Jane,' he said to his wife playfully; 'for really they look so much alike that I am quite sure I should not be able to tell one from the other.'

'You would if you had to wash and dress them,' she said.

'Very likely I should,' he said; then, after a pause, added: 'but really, Jane, this is too great a task on you.'

'I shouldn't do it but for the pay,' she said; 'but you know, John, that is very acceptable just now.'

'Yes, I know,' he said, a little bit sadly. 'It seems very hard that I should be smitten down with illness just when I had got a commission to paint a picture, and just when money was needed so much.'

'Troubles never come singly,' she said gloomily. 'Ours have come in battalions.'

'And yet things might have been worse,' he replied with a smile. 'I shall soon be at work again now, and you in your new capacity will be able to keep the wolf from the door until the picture is completed, though I do grieve that you have to work so hard.'

'Don't trouble about me,' she said, her face brightening a little. 'I shall be able to manage for a month or two without any difficulty; and then, think of the money.'

'That's the pity of it,' he answered. 'It worries me that we have to think so much about money. I dread the idea of painting "pot-boilers."'

'The pot must be kept boiling all the same,' she answered; and then the subject dropped.

A few days later John Raynor crept feebly up to his garret studio, and tried to settle steadily down to work; but it was a great effort, and one that almost overmastered him.

So the days passed on, but the picture could

scarcely be said to grow. John remained in his studio seeing almost nothing of his wife or children. But he was able to do no work that was worthy the name.

Then came that fatal afternoon on which our story opens. John had been so disheartened with his attempts to work that he could scarcely touch his dinner.

'I'm afraid I shall never succeed with the picture' he said gloomily, as he rose from his seat to retrace his steps to his workroom.

'Not succeed?' she questioned, looking up in surprise.

'I fear not,' he said; 'my hand seems to have lost its cunning.'

'Oh! I hope not,' she replied. 'It must be because you are still weak and worried.'

'Perhaps you are right,' he said. 'But it is very disheartening, nevertheless.'

When he had gone she sent the older children into the garden to play, and then, dropping into her rocking chair, she sat for a long time staring into the empty grate. Life seemed very hard, and the outlook dark in the extreme.

Suddenly a sharp cry from the gilded cradle startled her out of her reverie, and with a look of alarm upon her face she rushed to the corner and took the child up in her arms, and then dropped again into her rocking chair.

She saw that something serious was the matter,

though she never dreamed of it having a fatal termination. The attack, which proved to be one of syncope, was but of short duration. Almost before she knew what had happened, the child lay still and lifeless across her knees.

For a moment she was too horrified to move or even to speak. Then thoughts began to chase each other through her brain at lightning speed, and a terrible picture of pain, poverty, and reproach rose up before her.

Would Squire Brown believe she had taken proper care of his child? Would he not charge her with neglect, and in his grief and disappointment might he not say cruel things which would rankle in her heart to the end of her life?

And then there was his young wife. It would mean death to her. All her hope of life had centred in this little babe. For its sake she had held on to existence with a tenacity that had surprised the doctors. But she would die now; the link that bound her to earth was broken. When they conveyed to her the tidings that her baby-boy was dead, it was easy to predict what would happen.

'Oh, I know the shock will kill her,' Jane Raynor said to herself, 'and then they will blame me!'

Then she began to think of her own future. The two guineas a week for nursing the baby would cease now, and her husband was still unable to

work. What should she do? There seemed
nothing before them but starvation. What a prospect for her youngest born! Poor little waif!
It had come into a world of want and privation.
Better it had never been born.

Jane Raynor's face grew hard at the thought.
Her faith in Providence had been very feeble for a
long time past. A thousand things, it seemed to
her, were not as they ought to be. Why had this
child died? For God to take the child of the rich
and leave the children of the poor seemed to her
a terrible blunder. Nay, in the present case, it
seemed a cruel wrong, for the young mother's life
was trembling in the balance, and a thousand
beautiful hopes would be shattered by this blow.

If God had taken *her* child instead, bitter as
would have been the grief, she would scarcely have
complained. In the present circumstances—with
her husband almost helpless, and the future so dark
and hopeless—it would have been a merciful Providence. But to take this child, for whom there was
plenty—to dash its father's long-cherished hope, to
end the frail young mother's life, and to rob her
and her husband of the pittance on which they
were living at present—that seemed not merely a
mistake, but a wrong.

Then a cry from her own child arrested her
thoughts for a moment, and she looked down into
the poor wicker cradle at her feet, while a pitiful
smile stole over her face.

'My poor bairnie,' she said, half aloud, 'I don't know what is to become of thee. Poverty and want must be thy portion always.'

And for answer a smile stole over the infant's face, and it dropped asleep again.

Then a terrible suggestion stole into Jane Raynor's heart, which swept all the blood from her face and left her pale to the lips. She glanced swiftly round the room, for she seemed hardly certain that someone had not spoken to her. But no one was near. She was alone with the two babes.

But the voice was still in her heart, and the suggestion was repeated again.

'Why should the young mother die?' the voice said, 'and why should you and your children starve? Why should Squire Brown be left childless, and all his money go to strangers? And why should your babe grow up in poverty and want? Is not your child as good as his; and has it not as good a right to the pleasant things of life? The Squire would never know, nor would his wife! You have only to say the child upon your knee is your own, and place your own in the gilded cradle, and all will be straight and clear. You will save the Squire's hopes from being shattered, and spare to him his wife. You will provide for your own offspring, and be even paid for nursing it.'

'But it is not right!' Jane's conscience protested.

'Well, then, do the right,' said the tempter, 'and see what comes of it. You will kill the Squire's wife, and leave him a widower as well as childless. You doom your own child to poverty, and yourself to want and privation.'

'But I cannot do such a wrong,' she said, half aloud, with a wild, strange look in her eyes.

'Well, then, don't,' the tempter mocked, 'and be prepared for all the wrong that will follow — the reproach of the Squire, the knowledge that you might have saved his wife and didn't, the pangs of hunger you might have averted and wouldn't do it.'

'Oh dear,' she moaned, 'I don't know what is right.'

'Of course you don't,' said the tempter; 'nobody does. Right and wrong are inextricably mixed up. Circumstances alter cases. What is right to-day may be wrong to-morrow. Perhaps the nearest approach to right is that which means the greatest good to the greatest number.'

'If that be so,' she moaned, 'my duty is clear. But, oh, I do not know. I seem to have lost my way in the dark. I ought to know what right is— but it seems all wrong at present; while wrong is full of promise and hope.' So she battled with herself. But she asked help of no one—not even of God

CHAPTER II.

THE WRONG ROAD.

*'Sow truth if thou the True wouldst reap ;
Who sows the false shall reap the vain ;
Erect and sound thy conscience keep ;
From hollow words and deeds refrain.'—Bonar.*

THERE is an old proverb which says, 'He who hesitates is lost.' And, like many another old proverb, it contains a measure of truth. It is not, however, the whole truth. In some cases 'he who hesitates is saved.' The fool is lost because he will not hesitate or give himself time to think. Jane Raynor hesitated over-long. Had she acted at once, before the devil of selfishness and policy had had time to bewilder her brain, we should have had a very different story to tell, or perhaps no story at all. But she gave willing ear to the voice of the tempter, and listened to all his suggestions, and the longer she listened the more bewildered she became, and the more densely beclouded grew her moral sense.

And yet, paradoxical as it may sound, could she

have hesitated longer she might have been saved.
Given longer time, and her judgment might have
recovered its balance, and conscience secured once
more its authority. But she had to act when her
brain was most confused. Ere conscience could
reassert itself the deed was done.

Later in the day an inward voice kept repeating,
'Dare you presume to mend God's work? Do the
right, and leave the consequences with Him.' But
she had done the deed then, and the step she had
taken was irrevocable—at least, it seemed so to her.
Had she wished, she hadn't the courage to retrace
her steps. The mental and moral struggle she had
passed through, though it seemed to her to have
lasted a long time, had in reality lasted only a few
minutes. The mind works rapidly in moments of
strong excitement. The babe upon her knee was
still quite warm.

In after-days she never had a clear recollection of
the sequence of events. She acted like one in a
dream, and yet she exercised a caution that was an
astonishment even to herself in the days that
followed.

A few moments after she had settled upon her
course of action John Raynor was aroused out of a
day-dream by hearing her voice calling from the
foot of the stairs in quick, startled tones:

'John, John, come quickly, baby has a fit.'
Instantly he dropped his brushes and palette and
rushed downstairs and into the sitting-room.

'Oh, John,' she exclaimed, without looking up; 'I fear it is all over!'

He came to her side without a word as she bent over the wicker-cradle, but he remained only a second. 'I will fetch the doctor,' he said, and hurriedly left the room.

Fortunately the doctor was at home, and, without a moment's delay, hurried off to the house, leaving John to follow more slowly. Of course he could do nothing; for the little waif was beyond his skill. But, as it was very evident the child had died from natural causes, he promised to give a certificate of death, and so save them from the worry and pain of an inquest.

'It's very sad, very sad indeed,' he said to Jane Raynor in sympathetic tones; 'but you must bear up for your husband's sake, and try to think it's all for the best.'

Then he walked across to the other cradle in the corner, and stood for a moment or two with his hands folded behind his back. 'The young banker seems all right,' he said at length, turning to Mrs. Raynor.

'They were both all right half an hour ago,' she said with a gasp; 'it is terribly sudden.'

'Yes, yes,' he said a little absently; 'but such things will happen—will happen.' He had a habit of repeating the last words of a sentence, sometimes more than once.

Jane Raynor did not reply, and the doctor took

up his hat and gloves and stole quietly out of the house.

'It's well it's her child,' he muttered to himself, as he strode away in the direction of Elmwood, the handsome residence of Jonas Brown, Esq. 'If it had been the other child it would have killed Mrs. Brown—killed her.' And he slackened his pace a little while he pulled on his gloves. 'I must try to get the banker interested in the case,' he said half aloud. 'She ought not to have too much worry while she is nursing that child. He might pay for the burial of the infant; it would be nothing to him—nothing to him.'

And he quickened his pace again. It was a lovely afternoon in late April, with just enough edge on the wind to make walking a pleasure. The sky was almost cloudless, and in the plantations, which were just beginning to burst into green, the song of the thrush rose clear and sweet.

Ten minutes' brisk walking and Dr. Moffat passed through the lodge gates of Elmwood, and a moment later came face to face with the banker. Jonas Brown was a man of about forty-five, rather below the medium height, stout and florid. His face was not by any means prepossessing; it narrowed upward, as though nature had been trying a new pattern, and not with the most satisfactory results. His extremely heavy jaw and square chin seemed out of all proportion with his narrow, retreating forehead. His eyes were small and set close together. His nose short and thick, his voice husky.

On catching sight of the doctor he hurried forward at once. 'Glad to see you, doctor,' he said, shaking his hand. 'I'm always glad to see you these days, though I think Mrs. Brown is going on very well.'

'That's right,' said the doctor. 'I'm glad to hear it—glad to hear it.'

'Though I may tell you honestly,' went on the banker, 'I shall be very glad when we've seen the last of you.'

'Ah, that's always the way,' said the doctor with a smile—'always the way.'

'Sounds ungrateful, don't it?' the banker said with a laugh.

'Well, you see, we've got used to it,' said the doctor, still smiling. 'But, by-the-bye, I've just come from the Raynors'.'

'You have?' the banker questioned hurriedly. 'And the boy? Is he still going on all right? I wouldn't have anything 'appen to that boy for the world.'

The letter 'h' was the banker's Shibboleth, and he occasionally made sad work with it.

'The child is quite well—quite well,' said the doctor; 'but a sad thing has happened to Mrs. Raynor's own child.'

'Indeed!' questioned Mr. Brown, looking interested.

'Yes; it was seized with an attack of syncope, and died in a few seconds.'

'Died?'

'Yes; it was quite dead when I arrived.'

'Good heavens! If it had been my child, doctor! Think of it.'

'I have thought of it, and from every point of view it seems a great mercy it was their child, and not yours.'

'I should think so,' said Mr. Brown, growing very red. 'Why, doctor, think of it; there ain't no comparison.'

'And yet I feel very sorry for the Raynors,' said the doctor; 'they are very superior people. But I fear they are very hard pressed for money just now. Even the cost of burying the child will be a great tax upon them.'

'Why, look here, doctor: I'll bear the expense myself,' said the banker, in a sudden fit of generosity. 'I think I ought to do something, perhaps as a kind of thank-offering, that it wasn't my boy, don't you see.'

'Well, yes, it would be a gracious thing for you to do under the circumstances,' said the doctor, with a smile—'a very gracious thing.'

'Then I'll do it if you say so; and, what's more, I'll do it well. It shall have a brick grave, there now; for, good 'eavens! doctor, don't you see it might have been mine.'

And so it came about that the banker's child

was buried at the banker's expense, though he was not at the funeral, and when the little grave was filled in, the Raynors returned silent and tearful to their home, and life went on, to all outward appearance, as it had gone before.

Yet to Jane Raynor life could never be the same again. She saw clearly enough now that she had sinned, and sinned deeply, and yet she would not entertain the idea of attempting to rectify the wrong she had done. On the contrary, she tried day by day to justify her conduct to herself, and by persistent and determined effort she succeeded very largely in stifling the voice of conscience.

The most difficult thing of all was to receive money from the 'Squire'—as they generally called him—for nursing her own child. By no process of reasoning could she persuade herself that that was right, and yet it was inevitable—it was the earliest penalty of her wrong-doing. But she dwelt as little on that part of the transaction as possible. It was more satisfactory to her to think of the Squire's delight in the steady recovery of his wife, and the growing strength of his boy.

'I have done no harm to anybody,' she kept saying to herself. 'I have saved the life of his wife and made them both happy, and provided for baby's future into the bargain, and how that can be wrong it is difficult to see.' But she knew she had done wrong, all the same.

If it was a wrong to no one else, it was a cruel

wrong to herself. But she tried not to think of
that. She felt that she had suffered moral damage
and deterioration. She found no comfort in prayer
as once she had done, and when she read the Bible,
instead of finding inspiration as in the old days, it
kept constantly stabbing her with a nameless pain.
And so she put the Bible aside and scarcely ever
turned its pages, and prayer was never resorted to
either for comfort or guidance.

Her husband was quick to note the change in
her, but attributed it to totally different causes.
'This constant strain and anxiety are too much for
her,' he said to himself again and again. 'I do
wish I could free her from all care and worry, then
perhaps her good looks would come back again.'

She hardly seemed the same person he had
married ten years before: the bright-eyed, merry-
looking maiden was but too surely growing into a
hard-featured, unsympathetic-looking woman. She
rarely, if ever, laughed now, and, worse still, seemed
quite indifferent to his caresses.

'Of course the death of her baby is a great blow
to her,' he thought. 'But she will get over that in
time.'

He could not grieve for the child himself. He
had seen so little of it that it had had no opportunity of getting hold of his heart. Moreover, they
were so poor just now, that its removal seemed a
mercy rather than otherwise. Hence the little
grave in the churchyard soon slipped out of his

thoughts. His trouble was not for the dead, but for the living.

Meanwhile, little Reginald—which was also the name of the dead child—continued to grow apace, and to delight the household with his infantile ways. John felt himself growing so fond of the little fellow that he knew it would be a pain to part with him when the time should come, while the mother anticipated the day with perfect dread.

Very slowly Mrs. Brown's strength came back to her. Sometimes for days and days on the stretch she would seem to make no headway at all, and Dr. Moffat and his assistant would be almost in despair. But she had youth on her side, and hope, as well as an intense desire to live for the sake of her babe; and so she falsified all the predictions of those who saw her constantly, and the tide of her life, which had ebbed out to its farthest extremity, began to flow in again. Slowly, it is true, and with many recoils, but still surely her strength came back, till at length the doctors rubbed their hands gleefully and declared that she was practically out of danger.

None outside the walls of Elmwood rejoiced so much in her recovery as did Jane Raynor. It seemed a justification of her own conduct, and yet, if the truth must be told, she felt grateful her recovery was so slow. The longer the young wife was invalided, the longer would she be permitted to nurse her own child.

And so the days passed on, all too quickly for Mrs. Raynor, and as the time drew near when she knew she would have to give up her child, her longing to keep it became more and more passionate and intense. She did not dream the babe would have held her heart so tightly, or that the pain of parting would be so bitter. Truly, sin's harvest had ripened quickly.

CHAPTER III.

'Could ye bless him, father—mother,
  Bless the dimple in his cheek?
Dare ye look at one another
  And the benediction speak?
Would ye not break out in weeping,
  And confess yourselves too weak?'—
                    Mrs. Browning.

THE joy of the young mother when at length the
doctor permitted little Rex to be brought to her
and laid by her side was not soon forgotten by
those who witnessed it. She had promised her
husband and the doctor that she would be quite
calm, that she would not excite herself in the least,
and she was quite sure it would not do her the
least bit of harm to have her babe for a few
moments by her side, and press its soft dimpled
cheek against her own. But how could the pent-up
love of the mother-heart be suppressed, when at
length the little warm bundle of life was laid close
to her bosom?

She tried to be calm, but every kiss she pressed
upon the dimpled cheek was like a great sob, while

her tears fell like rain upon the little face. Then
she pushed it a little from her, and looked at it
with eager, hungry eyes, as though she would
impress its every feature upon her memory. Then
with a low murmur, 'My darling,' she cried over it
again and almost smothered it with kisses.

Jane Raynor, who had stood by the bedside a
little bit awe-stricken at the magnificence of the
room, and visibly moved by the young mother's
transport of joy, sat down at length and hid her
face in her hands and began to cry.

It was a strange feeling that took possession of
her, and one the like of which she had never
experienced before. She could not help rejoicing
in the young mother's joy. The very pathos of it
made her weep, and yet through her heart there
shot a pang of jealousy that almost startled her.

What right had this woman to weep over the
babe and call him her own? He was not her child.
Her child was dead, and she was usurping a right
that did not belong to her.

For a moment, she was tempted to snatch the
child from her bosom and rush with him out of the
room, but she held herself in check with a firm
hand. This was a part of the penalty of her sin,
and she must abide by it.

Yet she was glad when the interview was over
and she found herself back again in her own little
sitting-room, with the child snugly asleep in his
cradle.

For several weeks after that she went every day to Elmwood, taking little Rex with her. Then came the time she had dreaded so long. The parting could no longer be delayed.

Mrs. Brown was seated by an open window in the large cool drawing-room. Outside the hot sunshine was shimmering on the green lawn, and flashing from the still waters of the trout-pool which lay beyond the garden fence. Scarcely a breath of air was stirring, but such as there was came into the room laden with the perfume of a myriad flowers.

'I have sent for you, Mrs. Raynor,' Mrs. Brown began, 'to say I have secured a nurse for baby, a most suitable woman in every respect. You will understand why I have done this. I feel I want my darling always near me.'

'Yes, I quite understand,' said Mrs. Raynor with a gulp.

'Of course, you will come every day until he can be weaned completely,' Mrs. Brown went on.

'Yes, I shall be glad to do that,' was the answer. 'It is hard to give him up. You can understand my feelings.' And Mrs. Raynor began to cry.

'I do sympathize with you very much,' was the feeling answer, and Mrs. Brown's own eyes became moist while she spoke.

'You are satisfied with what I have done, I hope,' Mrs. Raynor said at length.

'Oh yes, perfectly satisfied,' was the answer.

'Indeed, we do not know how to be grateful enough for all the care you have taken of our darling.'

'He filled my heart after death had made the gap,' she said with a sob. 'Life will be very lonely for awhile.'

'You must come and see him whenever you want to,' Mrs. Brown said consolingly, and then the interview ended.

For many a long day after that, and for many a sleepless night, Jane Raynor suffered the full penalty of her sin. She had said that life would be very lonely, but the reality was even worse than her anticipations. She missed the winsome face of her baby everywhere, and hungered for the caress of its soft chubby hands with unutterable pain

Yet even now no thought of retracing her steps ever entered her head, or if so she banished it at once. She still persisted to herself that she had acted for the best, and that in time she would reap the benefit, even though now she reaped only pain.

But even if she herself reaped no benefit at all, what advantages would not the child reap! While her other children would be badly fed and clothed and educated, this one would have everything of the best. And *perhaps*, some day, when he grew to be a man, and was rich and influential, she could tell him how she had plotted and suffered for his sake, and he out of his abundance would give her enough to keep her and her husband in comfort all the rest of their lives. This little hope would obtrude itself, try as she might to check it. But he who attempts to mend God's work is a fool for his pains, and the harvest of evil can never be good.

Jane Raynor began to imagine after awhile that she was not very welcome at the big house. Mrs. Brown was always friendly and pleasant; but the purse-proud banker was of different fibre, and when he happened to be at home she was treated by him, she fancied, with marked coldness.

In truth, Jonas Brown was anxious to put an end to her visits.

'We don't want common people ever on our doorstep, and constantly caressing our son,' he said to his wife.

'I don't think the Raynors are common people exactly,' she said deferentially.

'Not common!' he said, dropping his heavy jaw. 'Why, they've scarcely a sixpence to bless themselves with.'

'I know they are poor,' she answered.

'Just so; and we cannot 'ave such people ever hanging about. Besides, who can tell how she may influence the child.'

'Why, he's only a baby yet,' she said with a smile.

'And all the more impressionable,' he said. 'It's

been always a matter of regret to me that she nursed him so long.'

'Why, Jonas?' she said, 'I'm sure she was very good to him.'

'Possibly! But people grow on what they feed. Funny if he should take after her instead of you, wouldn't it?'

'Oh, nonsense,' she said.

'No, it ain't nonsense at all; and I would like her visits to cease. We can't be uncivil to the woman, but we must discourage her.' And Jonas marched pompously out of the room.

And so it came about that Mrs. Raynor's visits to Elmwood became less and less frequent. And even when she did call she did not always see her child. Sometimes he was out with the nurse, sometimes asleep and could not be disturbed, and when on rare occasions she was permitted to take him in her arms and kiss his dimpled cheeks with passionate love, he was quickly taken from her, and she had to return home with her heart's hunger unsatisfied.

It was a cruel cross for her—far more heavy than she had ever dreamed it would be—but she made no complaint. She locked up her secret and her sorrow in her heart and went her way, but not without the hope that her turn would come sometime in the future.

So the days sped on and lengthened into weeks, and the weeks grew into months, with little of change to mark their flight. In the home of the

Raynors, even with the severest economy, the pinch of want was sometimes keenly felt, and the outlook was as dreary and depressing as ever. But at Elmwood there was mirth and feasting, for the shadow of death which had so long hung over its young mistress had been taken away, while 'the boy,' to quote Mr. Brown, 'was growing to be a beauty.'

Nor did the banker go beyond the truth in that remark. A bonnier child was not to be seen anywhere, though after awhile the question 'who he took after' became a very perplexing one. The banker was fain to believe that he took after his side of the house. 'My family has dark eyes and 'air, just like Rex has,' he said, a statement no one could dispute, for the simple reason that Mr. Brown's family was an utterly unknown quantity. It was assumed that he had had parents, but whether they were living or dead no one knew, not even the banker himself. It was supposed he might have brothers and sisters, though no one had ever seen them. It was understood that he hailed from somewhere across the border, though he had never shown any disposition to return to the place of his birth. He had found his way to Liverpool thirty years before, with all his worldly possessions tied up in a blue-check pocket-handkerchief, had entered a cotton-broker's office as errand boy, had worked his way steadily up until he knew the business better than his master, had finally succeeded —though no

one knew exactly how—in elbowing his chief out of
the concern and installing himself in his place.

For a few years he had his finger in every 'cotton
corner' known, and literally 'minted' money—at
least, so it was said. But at length, getting tired
of 'cotton,' he, with one or two other capitalists,
started a bank, which was known as the 'Imperial
National and Cosmopolitan Banking Company.' It
was an 'unlimited' concern, but as it was understood there was any amount of capital at its back,
no one appeared to have any doubts respecting its
stability. Indeed, the demand for shares was
almost unprecedented, and for many years they
steadily rose in value.

A year or two later Mr. Brown purchased Elmwood, a comparatively modern mansion, situated in
one of the most picturesque parts of Cheshire, and
within easy reach of the clean and thriving town of
Barwich. For a long time Elmwood remained
without a mistress. Not that Mr. Brown was
averse to matrimony, or was insensible to the
charms of the opposite sex. On the contrary,
Mr. Brown was particularly anxious to take to
himself a wife, and to this end had pursued his
inquiries in many directions, and had succeeded
in obtaining numberless introductions.

But in spite of his immense wealth, the ladies
fought shy of him. They did not object to his
money: they objected to him. To be the mistress
of Elmwood might be an enviable position, but to

be the wife of Jonas Brown was not by any means an inviting prospect.

'It is not so much that he is ugly,' the ladies were heard to say, 'as that his manners are so detestable.'

At length, however, to everyone's surprise—and particularly to his own—he succeeded in persuading gentle May Dearden to accept his hand and his fortune, and very soon after she was duly installed as mistress of his home.

On the day she became his wife Jonas thought his cup of joy was full. But when little Rex was born he could scarcely contain himself. Following upon that, however, had been many anxious months, but at length the skies had cleared again, and now, to all appearance, there was nothing to disturb the serenity of his life.

Perhaps Jonas would have been a little better pleased if his son, in feature and complexion, had more favoured himself; but if so, he did not betray his disappointment. 'He takes after my family, my dear,' he said to his wife—'distinctly after my family.'

'I am glad to hear you say so, Jonas,' she answered, not knowing what other reply to make.

'You must admit he does not take after you. Not in the least, my dear. You have blue eyes and fair 'air, beautiful 'air, I admit, but fair. But my family are all dark.'

'So I have heard you say before,' she remarked.

' Yes, they are all dark except me,' he said, as he pushed his fingers through the bleached stubble that crowned his head. ' Rex is a Brown, every inch of him.'

' It doesn't matter much what he is so long as he is good,' she said ; and then the subject dropped, to be taken up again at some future time.

So the days and weeks sped on and lengthened into months, and the months grew into years, and the years dragged out their slow lengths, while the child grew into a youth, and the youth into a young man.

The Raynors left Barwich while Rex was but a child, and for many years had been completely lost sight of. The banker was glad of this. While they remained ' under his nose, as it were,' to quote his own expression, he felt in some measure bound to take an interest in them, and to help them if they were in need. But if they chose to betake themselves to other parts, he was not in any way ' obligated ' to find out their whereabouts.

Moreover, he did not grow more generous with growing years, nor did his temper, never very sweet, show any signs of improvement. The sight of Jane Raynor's sad, careworn face had been a constant source of irritation to him ; her very look seemed to him like a mute appeal for help: and he hated helping people. Why could they not help themselves as he had done ? The blessedness of giving was yet unknown to him, because he gave un-

willingly. And though on several occasions he
sent assistance to the Raynors, 'a kind of thank-
offering,' he said, 'for the care they had taken of
his son,' in his heart he begrudged it all the while.

Hence their removal from Barwich was a positive
relief to him, and most devoutly did he pray that
the place that once knew them might know them
no more for ever.

CHAPTER IV.

THE YEARS SPEED ON.

A few short years—and then these sounds shall hail
The day again, and gladness fill the vale;
So soon the child a youth, the youth a man,
Eager to run the race his father ran.'—*Rogers*.

THE story of Rex Raynor's early life may be told in very few words without doing it any injustice. It was as uneventful as such lives usually are, and much more lonely. No brother or sister ever came to keep him company, or share his joys and griefs. For years his foster-mother was his only companion and he her only pleasure.

At school he was noted only for his skill in drawing faces—an accomplishment which got him into endless trouble with the masters, but made him any number of friends among his fellows. For figures he had a decided dislike, while grammar he detested. This last fact was rather a satisfaction to Mr. Brown than otherwise.

'The boy takes after me,' he said, with a loud laugh. 'Never could bear grammar myself; nor

never could see the good of it, either. Folks knew
how to speak before grammar was ever invented.
Rex is a real Brown—takes after his father, as he
ought to.'

'But you are so good at figures, Jonas,' said his
wife, 'and Rex has no taste at all in that direction.'

'Oh, that'll come likely when he sees the use of
'em,' said Jonas. 'When he gets interested in business he'll get interested in figures ; it's always so.'

'Yes ; very likely you are right,' she said meekly ;
and then the subject dropped.

Of Rex's *penchant* for drawing very little was
said. With the banker it was evidently a sore point.

'It comes of that woman nursing him so long,'
he said irritably, and nothing would convince him
to the contrary.

As Rex grew older he discovered how much his
foster-father disliked to see his drawings, and so
prudently kept them out of sight. Yet it was a
real grief to the boy. Other people praised his skill
in this direction. Even the masters at the school,
while constantly blaming him for making sketches
on his slate when he ought to have been busy with
sums or dictation, admitted that he was decidedly
clever in the use of the pencil. But Jonas could
see nothing in it.

'It's a bad, idle habit you've got into,' he said to
the boy; 'and, mind you, I don't want to see no
more of it'

3

'All right, pa,' Rex answered meekly, with quivering lip, and then ran away to find the woman he called his mother, to pour into her ear the story of his trouble and disappointment.

She, kind heart, comforted him as a mother knows how.

'Bring your pictures to me, Rex,' she said; 'I shall be always pleased to see them. But if your father does not care for them, you need not tease him.'

So Mr. Brown was left in peace as far as Rex was concerned, but he could not altogether escape the subject.

One day he came home in a state of great irritation. He had met the head-master of the Grammar School just outside the lodge-gates, who at once launched out in praise of Rex's peculiar gift.

'That son of yours, Mr. Brown, is quite a genius with his pencil,' he said. 'I am most decidedly of opinion that he ought to take lessons in drawing, and I am surprised that you object to it.'

'Well, I do object to it,' said Mr. Brown shortly. 'Is not that enough?'

'Well, hardly, I should say,' was the answer. 'If Nature has endowed the boy with a particular gift, I think it ought to be cultivated.'

'Nature be hanged!' said Jonas angrily.

'No, Mr. Brown; excuse me——'

'No; I shan't excuse you or anybody else. Do you think I want my son to be a 'ouse-decorator?'

And Mr. Brown grew three shades redder in the face than was his wont.

The schoolmaster was somewhat disconcerted. Still, he did not forget that he was a schoolmaster, and as such he was not in the habit of yielding to anyone.

' I said nothing about your son being a house-decorator,' he said warmly ; ' no such thought ever passed through my mind.'

' I would as soon Rex painted doors as daubed pictures to hang on walls,' said Mr. Brown.

' I am sorry you take such a view,' said the schoolmaster in milder tones.

' You needn't,' said Jonas pompously. ' I know what I'm about, and I wish you to remember that Rex is the son of a gentleman.'

' Yes ; I—I—I wish you good-evening ;' and the schoolmaster turned quickly on his heel and marched away.

' I wonder what the fool was going to say,' Jonas muttered to himself, as he stood for a moment looking after the retreating figure. ' But no matter ;' and he walked away slowly towards his home.

' It's all through living with those Raynors so long,' he said to his wife, whom he stumbled across in the hall—' all through them. I knew how it would be.'

' What are you referring to, Jonas ?' she said, looking up with an expression of bewilderment in her eyes.

'I'm referring to Rex,' he said angrily, 'and to that detestable habit he's got of drawing everything he sees. But I'll put a stop to it;' and he ascended the stairs hurriedly to his own room.

A month later a private tutor had been secured for Rex, and so his daily walks to and from the Grammar School came suddenly to an end. This was a great trouble to him at first; but he soon got to be very fond of Mr. Stone, his new teacher; and as the latter was something of an artist himself, and was also fond of botanizing, the two took long rambles across the fields and through the woods and over the hills, and so combined instruction with pleasure.

Mr. Stone soon discovered Rex's peculiar bent; nor was he left in ignorance of Mr. Brown's horror of his son becoming 'a painter.' At first he was completely puzzled how to manage the lad. Rex seemed to have no wish to be undutiful, and yet, all unconsciously, his long-division sums grew into caricatures of men and women, and his copy-books became ornamented with pen-and-ink sketches of houses and cattle and trees.

'Come, come, Rex, this will never do,' said Mr. Stone; 'you will never get on with your lessons if you waste your time in this way.'

'I'm really very sorry,' said Rex, lifting his handsome face to his teacher 'I didn't mean to do it, but the figures came somehow.'

'But you shouldn't let them come,' said Mr. Stone.

But Rex only shook his curly head, as though he meant to imply that it was of no use his tutor talking.

' Well, suppose we compromise matters ?' Mr. Stone remarked, after a pause.

' What's compromise ?' Rex questioned, his bright eyes brimming with mischief and good-nature.

' Well, suppose I allow you two afternoons a week for drawing. Will you work hard with your other lessons all the rest of the time ?'

' Won't I just !' he said eagerly, his face aglow with pleasure. ' But what will father say ?'

' I don't know ; but if he complains I will explain to him how matters stand.'

But Mr. Brown did not complain ; he did not seem to interest himself further in the matter. He discovered that Rex was beginning to take an interest in figures, and so was satisfied. Perhaps he thought he had outgrown what he called his idle habit. Anyhow, the matter was allowed to rest.

So Rex worked hard at his grammar and arithmetic for the sake of having two full afternoons for drawing, and on the whole made satisfactory progress. For Mr. Stone he developed a genuine affection. The two had many things in common, and the bright, breezy afternoons they spent together in the meadows and in the woods sketching, were amongst the most delightful in Rex's life.

He did not show his pictures to his foster-father; he knew that to do so would only irritate him, and Rex had a genuine horror of giving anybody pain.

He did not seem to have a single ungenerous fibre
in his nature; if he could please people he was in
his element.

So month by month he grew in mind and body,
winning the love of all with whom he came into
contact. To Mr. Brown his growth was a marvel,
and his kindly disposition a constant rebuke.

'I have to admit he 'as a streak of Dearden in
him,' he said to his wife one day; 'he don't know
the value of money, and 'as no idea of looking after
number one. I believe the young simpleton 'ud
give the shoes off his feet if he thought somebody
needed 'em more than himself.'

'Yes, Rex is very generous,' she said, with a
pleased smile.

'Generous be hanged!' he said, growing very red.
'I call it thriftlessness; he don't know the value of
things.'

'He knows the value of some things,' she said
pointedly.

'I don't know what they are, then,' he said, with
a frown; 'but he's just like you in many ways. I
have to confess he's a mixture of Brown and
Dearden.'

'Well, I'm glad he's like me in something,' she
said, with a smile.

'Oh yes, I dare say,' he answered gruffly; 'but if
he don't alter he'll never know how to butter his
own bread!' And with this deliverance Jonas left
the room.

Rex was sixteen when he experienced his first great trouble. He was then a tall youth, taller than Mr. Brown, in fact; straight as a rule, and with a face clean cut as a piece of Grecian sculpture.

Coming home from a long ramble with Mr. Stone, he learned that his foster-mother had been taken seriously ill.

For several days she had been ailing, but had made light of it, saying she would be all right again in a day or two. That afternoon, however, she had fallen down in a dead faint, and had to be carried upstairs to bed, while a messenger had been despatched for Dr. Moffat with all possible haste.

Rex was by her bedside in a moment, and yet at the sight of her face he drew back with a little cry of surprise and pain. He had never seen her look like that before. Her face was so white and drawn, her eyes half closed, her lips almost colourless.

She opened her eyes at the sound of his voice and smiled sweetly.

'Oh, mammy!' he exclaimed, springing to her side; 'what is the matter with you?'

'I know not, darling,' she gasped in a faint whisper; 'I feel so very strange.'

'But you will soon be well?' he questioned in pleading tones.

'I hope so, darling, for your sake,' she said slowly.

'Oh yes; Dr. Moffat will soon have you all right

again,' he said cheerfully. And he bent down his head and kissed her, not once or twice, but many times.

'My bonnie boy,' she whispered, holding his face between her hands; 'you have been my life, my all.'

He did not know how much those words meant at the time; but afterwards he understood.

It was with a heavy heart he left the room at Dr. Moffat's request. He felt as though he was standing face to face with some great calamity. His very life was wrapped up in the gentle-hearted woman he called his mother, and if anything should happen to her he felt that all his world would be changed.

CHAPTER V.

BETTER OFF.

'Her life had many a hope and aim,
  Duties enough and little cares,
And now was quiet, now astir,
  Till God's hand beckoned unawares—
And the sweet white brow is all of her.'
                                    R. Browning.

WHEN Rex awoke next morning after a restless and troubled night, he was surprised to see his foster-father standing by his bedside. It was not once a year that Mr. Brown came to his room; hence at sight of him Rex sprang up with a start.

'Father,' he exclaimed, 'what is the matter?' But Mr. Brown did not speak for several seconds. He was evidently labouring under strong excitement. His large mouth worked uneasily. His eyes were red, his hair dishevelled.

Rex waited for him to speak with a terrible foreboding in his heart.

At last the words came, slowly, and in a voice so changed that Rex scarcely recognised it. 'Your mother, Rex, is——,' but he did not finish the sentence. He seemed utterly unable to speak the word.

'Is mammy worse?' Rex asked, all the colour stealing from his face, leaving him deathly pale.

'She is gone, Rex—gone!' he said in a hoarse whisper, and he sank into a chair and buried his face in his hands.

'Gone!' said the boy, with a bewildered look in his eyes; 'I do not quite understand.'

But Mr. Brown did not seem to heed. For several seconds he sat swaying himself to and fro, as though trying to overcome his emotion. Then lifting his head suddenly, he said: 'You have no mother now, Rex. She has gone away from us. They say she has gone to heaven. I don't know anything about that. I only know she has gone from us;' and he rose slowly to his feet and staggered out of the room.

For a long time Rex sat perfectly rigid, staring at the closed door, but seeing nothing. He knew the worst, but he was unable to realize it yet. He had been told that his mother was dead, but he could not comprehend its meaning. It seemed to him as though all his faculties were benumbed. He could not weep nor moan even. The blow had stunned him; the pain of it would come later on.

He got up at length and dressed in a dazed, mechanical way, then crept softly downstairs and into the darkened breakfast-room. A few moments later Mr. Stone came into the room accompanied

by Dr. Moffat. Mr. Stone took his seat at once at
the head of the table and began silently to pour out
the tea. Mr. Brown did not put in an appearance.
The meal was a strangely silent and oppressive one.
The little conversation there was was carried on in
the lowest whisper. Rex heard something about
'spasms of the heart,' but he paid little heed to it.
He was trying to realize the meaning of this great
silence and horror that had dropped down upon the
household.

There were no lessons that day; so, soon after
breakfast, he stole quietly out of the house and made
his way across the lawn and into the paddock beyond it; then he climbed the fence into a large field,
and by-and-by struck a footpath leading into and
through a wood that crowned the low hill beyond.
A mile or so beyond the wood was a little hamlet
that had outlived its day. It might have been a
thriving place once, before steam began to work its
revolutions. It was almost deserted now.

At the entrance to the wood was a stile, on which
Rex sat down and tried to think. It was as lovely
a May day as ever brightened the earth. All the
fields and hills were swept with the freshest green.
The woods had put on their best attire. In the
shadow of the hedgerows the dewdrops still
lingered and blazed like diamonds when the sun
touched them now and then. The larks rose up
from the tall grass, and twittered their loudest in
the deep-blue vault above.

But Rex heard nothing, saw nothing. The terrible fact was eating its way into his heart—his mother was dead—and he was trying still to grasp its meaning.

Suddenly he lifted his head and listened. From far away up in the wood came the sound of singing. A sweet, pure voice was warbling forth the strains of a familiar hymn they often sang in church. Very distinctly the words came echoing down through the shadowy aisles:

> ' Other refuge have I none,
> Hangs my helpless soul on Thee :
> Leave, ah ! leave me not alone ;
> Still support and comfort me.
> All my hope on Thee is stayed,
> All my help from Thee I bring :
> Cover my defenceless head
> With the shadow of Thy wing.'

He had heard the words many times before, and they had seemed meaningless till now. But in this great grief that had struck his heart to numbness they seemed strangely sweet and comforting. He felt for the first time in his life that when earthly friends failed there was a Friend above to whom he could go.

Leaning his head upon his hand he shed his first tears that day ; they came slowly and silently at first, like the beginning of rain after a long drought, but by-and-by his whole frame shook with sobs.

And still nearer came the singer, and clearer grew the song. But Rex did not lift his head or try to get out of sight. He knew the voice, and did not mind in the least Evelyn May witnessing his grief.

At length the singing ceased, and a few moments later a soft hand was laid upon his shoulder, and a voice close to his ear was saying : ' Why, Rex, what is the matter ?'

But he did not speak or even look up. He was still shaking with sobs.

Adjoining the stile was a gate half open, so she came through quickly and knelt at his feet.

' Is your mamma worse ?' she asked pleadingly. But he only shook his head.

' I am glad she is not worse,' she said in a relieved tone of voice.

Then Rex lifted his head, his large beautiful eyes swimming with tears. ' Mamma has gone away,' he said, choking back the sobs. ' She has gone to heaven.'

' Oh no, Rex !' the girl answered quickly in startled tones.

' Yes; she has gone away,' he said, trying to keep his lips from quivering. ' I have no mother now ;' and he turned away his head and swept his hand swiftly across his eyes.

For a long time no other word passed between them. They were in the shadow of the wood, and so did not feel the heat of the sun. Up in the tall trees the birds were trilling forth their jubilant songs as though there were no such things in the world as sickness, and sorrow, and death.

At length Rex spoke again. Numberless scraps of sermons and texts had been passing through his mind, and so he put the question to his companion :

'Do you think, Evelyn, I ought to be glad that mamma is better off?'

But the maiden did not reply. She thought of her own mother—all she had in the world—and wondered if she were taken could there be gladness any more for her.

'You do not speak, Evelyn,' Rex said at length, with a pleading look in his eyes.

I cannot answer your question, Rex,' she said, with averted eyes. ' I do not think I could be glad. She must be better off, we know that; but, oh! it is hard for you.'

' Hard !' he said, with a strange, far-away look in his eyes. ' I think I shall die, Evelyn.'

'Oh no,' she said gently. ' You are young, Rex. You are not like poor old Mrs. Parker, who has lost her husband.'

'I don't know Mrs. Parker,' he said, looking up with sudden interest.

'She lives down in Thorbrig,' the girl answered. ' She is very old and very poor, and her husband was buried last week; and she wants to die. Ma sent me down with a basket of food to her, and I have been reading to her a little.'

' And is she in very great trouble ?' Rex asked.

' Yes, very great; but she said the words I read to her gave her a great deal of comfort.'

'I wish you would read to me, Evelyn,' he said quickly.

'Then I will,' she answered. 'I will read the same Psalm I read to Mrs. Parker;' and she opened her little Bible and commenced: 'Bless the Lord, O my soul, and all that is within me bless His holy name.'

He sat with his elbows on his knees and his face in his hands while she read, and when the soft musical voice ceased he rose to his feet without speaking; but the despairing look had gone out of his eyes, and in its place was the light of hope.

A few minutes later they walked away together down the slope of the sunny field, and parted in silence at the paddock fence.

But Rex could not trust himself that day to look upon the dear face he loved so much. On the following day, however, when she lay in her coffin, he stole noiselessly into the darkened room and sat for nearly an hour looking at the sweet still face. It helped him to realize what he had failed to realize before. And somehow, while he wept silently and without restraint, 'the ache,' as he called it, came slowly out of his heart, and in its place there entered the calm of resignation.

Yet life could never be the same at Elmwood again. The gentle, sad-eyed woman who had ruled its fortunes for so many years was missed everywhere, and missed more and more as the days sped on.

People said Jonas Brown was never the same after his wife's death, nor is that much to be wondered at. She was the one refining influence that touched his life. She had held in check the coarser side of his nature, and had helped to develop whatever there was in him of kindness or charity. But now she was gone he was completely adrift. He had loved her as he had loved nothing else in the world save his money, had deferred to her at times to an extent that was an astonishment to himself. He was like a kite overweighted, yet while she held the cord he soared a little, though never to any great height; but when her hand relaxed its hold he quickly fluttered downward, and never made an attempt to rise again.

Had she known how much she helped him, and from what she saved him, it would have been an added touch of pleasure to her comparatively joyless life. She had never loved him, though she had tried her best. She had married him partly for his money, but mainly to punish another, and only discovered her mistake when it was too late. She did not know how coarse and selfish he was till she came to live with him, and when she found it out it nearly broke her heart.

But for Rex, she would not have cared to live at all. He was the light of her eyes, the joy of her life. And doubtless it was well that she passed quietly away into the Silent Land ere the discovery was made that he was not her own.

CHAPTER VI.

CHANGES.

'Fortune, that with malicious joy,
  Does man, her slave, oppress,
  Still various, and unconstant still,
  Promotes, degrades, delights in strife,
  And makes a lottery of life.'—*Dryden.*

Two years later Jonas Brown brought a new
mistress to preside over the fortunes of Elmwood.
He could never explain satisfactorily even to himself why he had done so. His marriage had been
a surprise to him in both instances, but in different
ways. Years ago he had been surprised that
May Dearden should marry him; now he was
equally, if not more, surprised that he should
marry Mrs. Rudd. To begin with, he did not
particularly want a wife, and, furthermore, he was
not particularly fond of Mrs. Rudd. She was a
tall, handsome woman, large and stately, with a
loud voice and a haughty, overbearing manner.
She rather overawed Jonas, and after his marriage

4

he had a feeling that he had been wheedled into it against his will.

Perhaps he was right. Mrs. Rudd had resolved soon after May Brown had been buried that she would become the mistress of Elmwood. In this resolve she was aided and abetted by her two daughters, Joyce and Julia. In fact, Joyce had informed her mother that if she did not marry Mr. Brown she (Joyce) would do so herself, as she considered it a shame that such a place as Elmwood should be left without a mistress when there were so many eligible widows and spinsters who wanted homes.

Mrs. Rudd commended her daughter for displaying so much worldly wisdom. ' But you must remember, Joyce,' she added, ' that having had three husbands already, I'm no novice, and may be trusted to look after myself.'

' Yes, I think you may,' Joyce answered sententiously, while Mrs. Rudd glided out of the room in her stateliest manner.

In angling for Mr. Brown Mrs. Rudd displayed uncommon skill, but the end she considered amply justified the endeavour. It was a proud day for her when she entered Elmwood as its mistress, a proud day also for her daughters. For several years they had had more than enough to do to make both ends meet, and such a battle with poverty had been very humiliating. That was at an end now. While Joyce and Julia, as the step-daughters of the rich banker, would stand a much better chance in the matrimonial market.

Rex could barely conceal his disappointment, not to say disgust. This loud-voiced, overbearing woman was so different in every respect from the gentle creature he had called 'mother' that he turned away from her with something like a shudder. Nor was he much better pleased with the two J.'s —Joyce and Julia. He had an artist's eye for neatness and harmony and beauty in everything, and these loud-dressed girls were an offence to him.

He could not be other than civil and polite to them, but he knew from the first he would never take to them nor they to him.

Rex was eighteen at the time—tall, well-knit, handsome, with a manner so gentle, and yet so chivalrous, that he won nearly all hearts, and with grace and strength in every movement.

Everyone who knew Mr. Brown was astonished that he should have so handsome a son.

'Can't understand it for the life of me,' said Mr. Leslie, the Vicar, when visiting Mrs. May, Evelyn's mother, one afternoon. 'Brown is as ugly as sin, and Rex is as handsome as an Apollo.'

'Yes, he is very handsome,' Mrs. May answered, while Evelyn bent her eyes lower over her sewing.

'And then he's so gentlemanly and graceful while Brown waddles like a duck.'

'That is his misfortune, Mr. Leslie,' Mrs. May said with kindly rebuke.

4—2

'Yes, yes, I don't deny that,' went on the Vicar; 'I am simply showing how unlike the son is to the father. And then Rex is quite artistic, you know.'

'Yes, I know; and Mr. Brown doesn't care for pictures, I think.'

'Care for them? Why, he doesn't know a picture from a pancake.'

Mrs. May laughed, then added: 'Perhaps his new wife will teach him.'

'Teach him?' he answered, with a shrug of his shoulders; 'well, yes, I fancy she will teach him many things, but not that;' and then, after slyly hinting that he would be glad if Mrs. May would occasionally come to church, the Vicar took his departure.

Mr. Leslie's surmise, however, was quite correct. Mrs. Brown did teach her husband many things. In less than three months he had learned more about domestic economy than all his life before he had ever dreamed of. Indeed, before she had been mistress of Elmwood a week she began to take the reins into her own hands.

'This house has never been properly managed,' she said to her daughter Joyce. 'And if there is one thing I pride myself on it is on knowing how to manage. Mr. Brown shall soon see what management can do.'

Mr. Brown did see, to his sorrow. The expenses of housekeeping were doubled in an incredibly

short space of time, while comfort had been reduced to a decimal.

At length he ventured a complaint—a very mild
one, it is true. But Mrs. Brown came down upon
him like an avalanche.

'I'm surprised at you,' she said, with a toss of her
stately head; 'you, a rich banker, and wishing to
starve your family.'

'No, my dear,' Jonas remonstrated.

'Call me Mrs. Brown, please,' she said with lofty
condescension; 'and understand I'm not used to
such cheese-paring. In my first husband's time,
good man——'

'Ah, a pity he ever died,' muttered Jonas, in a
sudden blaze of anger.

'What's that you say?' she demanded loftily, but
Jonas discreetly kept silence.

'Well, understand I intend to live as becomes my
station,' she said; 'dinners you shall give, whether
you like it or not; and dances for young people
the girls have determined upon.'

'The girls be hanged!' thundered Jonas, unable
longer to restrain himself. Mrs. Brown stepped
back a pace or two in speechless horror.

'Do my ears deceive me?' she said at length.

'I hope not,' was the surly reply.

Mrs. Brown sat down and began to fan herself.
Jonas stood with his back against the mantelpiece
looking fierce and defiant.

'Does this mean war?' she said at length.

'I don't know,' he said; 'I would rather have peace.'

'In which case,' she answered a little more mildly, 'we had better understand each other.'

'Well?' he grunted interrogatively.

'Well, there are a few things I would like to say.'

'Say on,' he said in a surly tone.

'Then I wish you to understand, Mr. Brown, that I *must* be mistress in my own house.'

'Your house,' said Jonas reflectively.

'Yes, my house. This is my domain, and I wish to say I will not have that son of yours, who is a prig——'

'My son is a Brown,' ejaculated Jonas, with a sudden rise of temper.

'Yes, he is a *Brown*,' she said, with a curl of the lip.

'And a gentleman,' thundered Jonas.   •

'Singular,' she answered, with provoking scorn —'a Brown and a gentleman. But be it so. I will not have this gentleman wasting his time here. He must go to business, do you hear?'

'Go to business?' he questioned; 'I intend him to go to Cambridge.'

'Stuff and nonsense,' she said; 'he is old enough to be doing something for himself. Besides, it will keep him out of mischief.'

'But there is no need,' he said; 'I intend Rex to be a gentleman.'

'There are plenty finer gentlemen than he in

business,' she said; 'and you must find room for him in the bank. I will not have him loitering about here any longer.'

And Mrs. Brown rose from her seat and walked with stately grace out of the room.

The fight, however, did not end there. It was renewed again and again. But in the end Mrs. Brown carried her point.

Rex raised no objection at all. In fact, he was rather pleased than otherwise. It would be a change, if nothing else, and a change was particularly welcome just then. He was sick of the society of the two J.'s, and disgusted with the haughty airs of Mrs. Brown.

It is true he had no fondness for figures, but he settled down to his work, nevertheless, with a dogged determination to do his best, and found the journey to and from Liverpool, morning and evening, a pleasant break in the monotony of his life. In fact, the change did him good every way. The habit of punctuality, the necessity of going into detail, the interchange of ideas, the close and daily contact with men and things, all tended to quicken and develop his latent energies.

Moreover, there was always something to be seen and learnt in the city. Exhibitions of pictures, lectures on art and science, sacred and secular concerts, literary and debating societies, all of which possessed for him a wonderful charm.

So that during the winter months he generally

spent two evenings a week at least in the city,
returning by the last train to Barwich. At Elmwood he had the old schoolroom fitted up as a
' den ' for himself. Here he kept his books, fishing
tackle, and artist's tools. Here on summer morn-
ings he would spend an hour or two in working up
his sketches, while on winter evenings he would
enjoy alone the newest book.

This order, however, was occasionally varied by
a visit to Beechlawn, the beautiful home of Evelyn
May and her mother, and sometimes when the
weather was fine he would ramble with Evelyn
across the fields on some sketching excursion.

Since the death of his foster-mother no one had
taken such kindly interest in his welfare as Mrs.
May, nor was there anyone to whom he could open
his heart so freely, except, perhaps, to Evelyn.
She seemed like a sister to him—at least, so he
thought and believed. She was only about a year
younger than he, and as he had known her nearly
all his life, it was only natural that their intercourse
should be free and unrestrained.

Mrs. May could see no impropriety in Rex and
Evelyn being so much together. Evelyn, in her
mother's eyes, was only a child yet, and Rex seemed
to her but an overgrown boy—a bright, handsome,
chivalrous boy—whose coming was always like a
gleam of sunshine, and whose merry laughter was
like music in her large but quiet home. So the
young fellow went and came at will. If ever he

had a fit of the blues, or was particularly bored by the two J.'s, he would escape from the house at the first opportunity and hie away to Beechlawn, sure of a kindly welcome, and sure of company that would give him pleasure.

CHAPTER VII.

A REVELATION.

'I would not waste my spring of youth
In idle dalliance ; I would plant rich seeds
To blossom in my manhood, and bear fruit
When I am old.'—*Hillhouse.*

WHEN Rex was twenty-one he was the envy of
nearly all the young men of his acquaintance. He
was handsome, healthy, and rich. What more
could any young man desire ? And yet, as if that
were not enough, he was beloved by all whose love
was worth possessing; was respected by hundreds
who had no personal acquaintance with him; and,
to crown all, was living a life of daily usefulness
and help. And yet he was not altogether satisfied
nor by any means completely happy.

The place he called his home was altogether
lacking in that feeling of ' homeness' which he so
much desired. There was no one there to greet
him with a smile of welcome on his return from
business, no one to share his hopes or pleasures.

He had his own rooms, and came and went as though he had been a lodger.

Perhaps he was himself partly to blame for this. He shrank instinctively from Mrs. Brown and her two daughters, and they were quick to notice and resent. When he sought the privacy of his own ' den ' they did not seek to intrude ; and when they gave their parties they did not invite him to join in the dance.

And so he lived like a stranger among strangers, and sought his pleasures outside the circle of his home.

Between himself and the man he called his father there never had been any sympathy, and as the years passed on the two seemed to drift farther and farther apart. When they went into the city they never travelled by the same train ; and, with the exception of Sundays, they rarely sat down together to the same table.

Of late Mrs. Brown and the two J.'s had helped to poison Mr. Brown's mind and to increase his prejudice against his son.

'I wish your son knew how to behave,' Mrs. Brown said to her husband one morning over the breakfast-table.

' Yes, he's a perfect bear,' broke in Julia.

' Why, what has he been doing now ?' asked Mr. Brown.

'It isn't so much what he does as what he doesn't do,' interposed Joyce.

'Yes, that's just it,' said Julia; 'he's so awfully good—he might be graduating for a saint.'

'What a pity you didn't bring him up to be a clergyman, Mr. Brown!' Mrs. Brown remarked, with a curl of her proud lip.

'Or a dissenting minister,' interjected Joyce.

'Yes; he really ought to join some religious brotherhood,' said Julia. 'Think of it, he never came into the ball-room the whole of last evening.'

'Perhaps he didn't know what was going on,' said Mr. Brown gruffly; 'I don't expect you consulted him.'

'Consulted him, no! what's the use? he lives in too exalted an atmosphere to care for such things.'

'If that quaker Miss!—Evelyn May—had been here, he would have showed up quick enough,' said Joyce.

'No doubt, but I wonder why she did not come?' said Julia; 'she has come to our parties before.'

'Oh, her mother thinks her too good for this sinful world,' said Mrs. Brown, with a toss of her head; 'but I think you did very well without her.'

At this point Mr. Brown rose from the table and left the room. In truth, he was getting sick of such conversations, and yet they were not without their influence upon him; all unconsciously he was getting more and more prejudiced against Rex.

'Wish the young fool 'ud be like other folks,' he muttered as he struggled to get into his overcoat.

At the door the brougham was waiting to take him to the station.

'Have the horses been out before this morning, Sparks?' he asked the coachman.

'No, sir,' said Sparks, touching his hat: 'Master Rex preferred to walk.'

'Just like him,' muttered Jonas as he stepped into the carriage; 'he won't be like other folk; we shall never make a gentleman of 'im.'

Later in the day they met in Mr. Brown's private office.

'Look 'ere, Rex,' Mr. Brown said, getting up from his chair and pushing the door to; 'I've got something to say to you.'

'I'm at your service,' Rex answered quietly.

'Well, then, I want to know why the—that is, why, in the name of common-sense, you don't behave decently.'

'Behave decently?' Rex questioned, raising his eyebrows in astonishment.

'Yes; why can't you behave like other young men, and treat your sisters with proper respect?'

'I am not aware that I ever treated them otherwise than with respect,' Rex answered.

'They tell me you never showed up at the dance last night,' Jonas replied, 'and that you rarely ever do.'

'I did not get home till late last night,' Rex answered, 'and I did not know there was a dance till after I got home. Besides, I was busy over a lesson for my class.'

'Your class be hanged!' said Jonas, growing very red. 'That's the kind of thing I object to.'

'I don't see why,' said Rex firmly. 'I've nearly a hundred young men whom I am trying to instruct. I see no harm in that.'

'You don't, don't you? Well, I do; I hate such Socialistic ways.'

'I don't know what you mean by Socialistic ways,' said Rex, growing a little pale.

'Why, I mean you are teaching 'em Socialism— the Vicar thinks so, too—teaching 'em as all men are equal; and I don't believe in it.' And Mr. Brown took two or three turns round his office.

'We do read the New Testament sometimes,' said Rex, with a mischievous smile. 'That is rather a Socialistic book, isn't it?'

'Well, I don't know but what it is, now you mention it,' said Jonas, running his fingers through his bleached stubble. 'I never thought of it before, but I believe it is. I'll ask the Vicar about it.'

'What good will that do?' Rex questioned.

'Good be hanged!' snarled Mr. Brown. He always wanted to hang everything that came in his way.

'Well, no, I would not go so far as that,' said Rex, with a smile.

'I wish you'd go a deal farther,' growled Jonas.

'In what way?'

'Why, in behaving like a gentleman. Why can't you drink your bottle of champagne at dinner sometimes, and go to the races, and mix with folks that are your equals? Giving up your time to a lot of artisans, as you do, is demoralizing, I call it.'

'I must beg to hold a different opinion in regard to that matter,' said Rex firmly.

'Oh yes, I dare say,' snarled Jonas; 'you never agree with me in anything. What with your painting, and your philanthropy, and your high-falutin' notions, I don't know what is to become of you; and who you take after is a mystery to me.'

'I am sorry I do not please you better,' Rex said, after a pause; 'but I cannot be what you wish.'

'Oh no; I dare say you'll go your own gait, and a pretty pass it'll bring you to in the end.' And Jonas opened the door while Rex bowed himself out.

'Just as I expected,' Jonas growled as he resumed his seat. 'The young fool will never be like other folks; I might as well talk to the door-post.'

Rex returned to his desk with a very perturbed feeling at his heart, and during the whole of the afternoon he was restless and ill at ease. As soon as the bank closed he made his way to the station and caught the earliest train to Barwich. He thought he would find solace in his books and pictures, but he was as restless in his 'den' as in the bank.

'It's of no use,' he said at length, starting to his feet. 'I'll go for a ramble, and make a call on my way back at Beechlawn.'

The early October afternoon was already beginning

to fade, and a thin gray mist was slowly creeping up the hillsides, softening the outlines of the distant trees. Under foot the crisp yellow leaves already lay thick, showing unmistakably that summer was past; while in the atmosphere there was that unmistakable chill which denotes the approach of winter.

Rex struck out at once for the Thorbrig footpath. He liked the ramble through the long plantation which crowned the slope, and he felt that this evening its shadowy aisles and deepening gloom would be in keeping with his mood.

At the stile, where years ago on a bright May morning he sat in his sorrow and Evelyn May came and comforted him, he paused for awhile, while memory gleaned among the stubble of bygone days. He always liked to think of Evelyn; she was so sweet, so gentle, so strong.

He had grown up with her from childhood, and had watched with delight the gradual unfolding of her mind and heart. Her beautiful face, he knew, was but the index of a beautiful soul. In her clear and steady eye no evil passion ever shone, and in her heart there seemed no room for guile.

Suddenly he started. From far up in the wood came the sound of voices and of low rippling laughter. Then two dusky figures appeared in sight, and sauntered leisurely towards the stile. It was getting quite dusk now, so he stepped aside that they might pass. He saw Stuart Leslie, the

"He stepped aside that they might pass."

Vicar's son, mount the stile, for the gate at the side was closed; then he reached his hand to his companion and helped her gently over, speaking low the while.

Rex bit his lips, and drew farther back in the shadow of the hedge. A moment later Stuart Leslie and Evelyn May walked away together down the long slanting field, and were soon lost among the gathering shadows. Then Rex leaped the stile at a bound and tore up through the wood, as though eager to make up for the time he had wasted.

He had been miserable enough before; he was a hundred times more so now. He felt as though something or somebody had stabbed him. The sight of Stuart Leslie helping Evelyn May over the stile had stirred up a latent fire which had been slumbering within him for years, and which for the moment dominated his whole being. Later in the evening he was able to reason the matter calmly with himself.

Perhaps their being together meant nothing. She had doubtless gone to see her old people at Thorbrig, as she often did, and had stayed a little later than usual. He had accidentally stumbled across her path when out for a ramble, and, as any gentleman would of her acquaintance, had promised to see her home. What was there for him to chafe about in that? Besides, she was nothing to him, or he to her. But stop!—was she nothing to him?

5

The revelation came to him like a flash—she was everything to him.

He did not go to Beechlawn that evening. His ramble ended, he returned to his own den and locked the door. A new problem was staring him in the face, and he was undetermined how to act. That he loved Evelyn May he had no doubt. But did she love him? Did she love another? This he must find out. And if he was to woo and win her he must begin at once. But perhaps he was already too late. He had heard for a long time past of Stuart Leslie going a great deal to Beechlawn, but he had thought nothing of that. It was a sweet, beautiful home, to which any young man with refined feelings might love to go, and would be all the better for going. He had never thought of Evelyn in the matter. Now everything came back to him with a rush.

While his own strong love had been slumbering, and he had been content to let things drift, the Vicar's son had stepped in before him, and perhaps had already won the prize.

And Rex clenched his fists· and paced the room in impotent anger and jealousy. He saw clearly enough that his rival, if rival he was, was a formidable one. He was well educated, refined, and good-looking; while his father being rich apart from his living, his prospects were exceptionally good. He might be lacking in depth of character, and was rather too much of ' the young man about town ' style to suit some folk. But that he could be very fascinating when he liked no one doubted who knew him; and Rex's great fear was that he had already pleaded with Evelyn and had prevailed.

But before he slept that night he had come to the resolve that he would know the truth at the first possible opportunity.

CHAPTER VIII.

FOREBODINGS.

'No haughty gesture marks his gait,
    No pompous tone his word,
    No studied attitude is seen,
    No palling nonsense heard ;
    He'll suit his bearing to the hour,
    Laugh, listen, learn, or teach ;
    With joyous freedom in his mirth,
    And candour in his speech.'—*Eliza Cook.*

REX did not go to Beechlawn on the following night, though he was impatient to know his fate. It was the night for meeting his young men, and so strong had become his conviction of duty in relation to this matter, that he would not let it stand aside for any other consideration.

He had commenced with a very small class at the Mechanics' Institute, and with no very clear ideas in his mind of what he might accomplish. He had plenty of time at his disposal, and if he could do any little good in the world he had a feeling that he ought to make the attempt, and so he started with half a dozen mere lads in his class, with the intention of taking them through a course of natural history.

But the interest grew wonderfully. His blackboard lessons became the talk of the town. His class-room, in a few months, was crowded out, and an adjournment was made to the lecture-room ; and even this, on special nights, became crowded to its utmost capacity.

For the winter in question he had made arrangements to give a series of lectures on such subjects as thrift, recreation, reading, health, ventilation, the morning tub, and many other kindred topics.

His own interest had deepened and intensified as time had gone on, until now it was one of the chief pleasures of his life to meet his young men, as he termed them, though many of them were old enough to be his father.

He had prepared his first lecture with great care. Indeed, he had mapped out the whole series and for months had been gathering materials for their completion. He little dreamed that the work begun so auspiciously would end in the manner it was destined to do. But events were ripening which cast no shadows before, and he went on from day to day recking not of what was coming.

It was with very mixed feelings he wended his way to the lecture-hall that evening. He was full of enthusiasm for his subject, and yet nervous to a degree that was most ususual with him. He had

not the smallest desire to shirk his work, and yet
all the while his thoughts were straying from it.

He had been awakened suddenly to the fact that
Evelyn May, whom he had known so long and had
looked upon almost as a sister, was more than any
sister could ever be. That she was, in fact, the very
light of his eyes and the hope of his life. But with
this awaking had come the fear, which had haunted
him ever since, and refused to be shaken off, that
the discovery had come too late, and that she had
given her love to another.

If Stuart Leslie loved her he could not wonder,
for who could be long in Evelyn May's company
without loving her? If she loved him, he had to
confess to himself there could be no cause of surprise. And yet the thought was torture to him.
She had grown so unconsciously, and yet so completely, into his life, that the bare idea of becoming
to her as a stranger and seeing another claim her
as his own was maddening.

He battled with the feeling as best he could, but
the fear was ever present with him. He saw the
possibility that while he was doing his best to
enlighten his young men on the question of thrift,
the Vicar's son might be at Beechlawn urging his
suit. But there was no fibre of cowardice in Rex's
heart, and with a manful effort he threw himself
into his work, and after awhile forgot everything
else in the subject he had come to discuss.

The gathering was a success in every sense of the

word. Rex's social position of itself was enough to secure him a respectful hearing. But much more than that, he was respected, nay, beloved, by all who came to listen to him. Then there was a charm about his manner—an easy grace of speech —that was sure to win attention, while, to crown all, he was master of his subject, and marshalled his arguments in a way that carried conviction at every point.

Few things are more contagious than the enthusiasm of a crowded meeting. Rex came under its spell quite at the beginning. In the very first sentence he caught the attention of his audience, and he held it to the end; while they, charmed by his oratory, yielded to its magnetism at once, and were swayed by it like a cornfield by a summer's breeze. How he could invest what they termed 'dry subjects' with so much living interest was always a puzzle to them. Arguments, anecdotes, and illustrations were so skilfully interwoven, that the address seemed like a piece of mosaic, full of gay colours, yet blending in perfect harmony.

Rex did not stay to listen to the compliments which his auditors were eager to pay him. He retired by a side door and made his way slowly homeward, and then locked himself in his den till bedtime. During all next day he was restless and ill at ease. He had resolved to know his fate before he slept, and yet, as the day waned, he almost feared to know.

Directly the bank closed at three o'clock he started for Barwich, and just as the day was closing he left Elmwood and made his way in the direction of Beechlawn. The residence of Mrs. May was beautifully situated, and surrounded by extensive and well-kept grounds.

Rex walked at a rapid rate until the house came into sight, then he slackened his pace and once or twice came to a dead halt, as though undecided whether to go farther or not; but if so, his hesitancy was not of any long duration.

During the day he had tried to frame a speech that should pave the way to the avowal he was wishful to make. Yet somehow every form of words seemed stilted and theatrical, and he could hit upon nothing that just suited his taste, or would express one half of what was in his heart; and so at length he came to the conclusion that he would trust to the chapter of accidents and say what came readiest at the time. Yet the nearer he got to the house the more difficult seemed the task he had set himself. The last day or two had changed everything. How often he had raced up that well-kept drive with all the freedom of a school-boy, and had plunged into the house as though it were his own home; much, it must be confessed, to the astonishment of old Thompson the butler, who had very strict notions of propriety.

Now, however, he was approaching the house as though he were a stranger and not at all sure of a

welcome. He seemed to have suddenly realized
that Evelyn was a woman and he a man, and that
the old days of unrestrained freedom had passed
away for ever, and, on the whole, the discovery was
not a very pleasant one. However sweet it was to
love, the fear that his love was not reciprocated
seemed far to outweigh the pleasure.

At length he paused and drew a long breath.
The carriage drive had wound round in front of
the drawing-room windows, and he found himself staring into that handsome apartment after a
fashion he would have deemed rude in anyone else.
But at the moment he was completely self-for-
getting. The picture he saw just charmed his
artist's eye, besides setting his heart throbbing
wildly.

Outside it was dark enough by this; but within
the blinds had not been drawn, nor had the lamps
been lighted. But in the large old-fashioned grate
a wood fire was crackling, and lighting up the room
with a soft warm glow, and decorating the polished
furniture with long streaks of vermilion.

Before the fire, on a low chair, sat Evelyn, her
hands clasped round her knees, her eyes fixed
intently upon the grate. On her strong, pure face
the firelight flickered and played, and danced in
the liquid depths of her lustrous eyes.

Truly she was no longer a girl. Rex felt that, as
he gazed at her, in a way he had never felt it
before. Her beautiful hair was twisted in a shining

coil at the top of her head, her well-rounded figure
stood out in clear relief in the soft warm light. She
had always been beautiful in Rex's eyes, but he
thought she never looked so beautiful as now.

How long he stood there he never knew. It
might have been only a few seconds, or it might
have been many minutes. He remembered wondering what she was thinking about, she sat so still
and with such a far-away look in her eyes. Could
it be possible she was thinking of him, or did the
Vicar's son fill her heart and monopolize all her
dreams ?

He started at length as a low wail of autumn
wind stole slowly through the trees and died softly
away in the distance.

'How rude I am!' he said to himself. 'If she
knew I had been staring at her in this way she
might never forgive me;' and he smiled a little,
then added, 'if she does not want to be looked at
she should have the blinds drawn.'

And with this reflection he mounted the door-
steps and rang the bell.

A moment later Thompson appeared and ushered
him into the hall.

'Mrs. May is engaged at present,' Thompson
explained; 'but Miss Evelyn is about somewhere.'

'Yes, she is in the drawing-room,' Rex said
quickly; 'I saw her through the window as I
passed.'

'Perhaps you will go to her,' said Thompson,

for Rex and Evelyn were still only boy and girl in
his eyes.

'Thank you, I will,' said Rex, and Thompson
prepared to lead the way.

'You need not trouble, Thompson,' he said with
a laugh; 'I think I know the way.'

'Well, yes, I think you do,' said the old man,
while Rex made his way with beating heart in the
direction of the drawing-room.

On reaching the door he paused for a moment
and drew a long breath; then, raising his hand, he
knocked gently on one of the panels.

'Come in,' was the answer, in a sweet, musical
voice that thrilled his heart like a psalm; and,
grasping the handle, he pushed over the door and
entered.

Evelyn was still seated, but when she saw who
her visitor was she rose from her chair in a moment,
and came to meet him with extended hand.

'What, Rex?' she said in a tone of surprise,
perhaps of disappointment; 'I thought perhaps it
—that is, I hardly expected you. Your visits have
been so few and far between of late.'

Rex's heart sank. 'It was not me she expected,
but another,' he said to himself; 'and she is disappointed he has not come.' But he controlled his
feelings by a manful effort, and answered some
commonplace about being very much occupied.

'Yes, I know you must be very busy,' she said
with a smile, 'so I suppose we must forgive you.

But won't you take a seat while I ring for lights ?'

He would have prevented her if he could. He would rather have talked to her in the firelight. But there was no help for it now. So he threw himself into an easy-chair and waited with as much patience as he could command for his opportunity to come

CHAPTER IX.

DISCOURAGEMENT.

'Our doubts are traitors,
And make us lose the good we oft might win,
By fearing to attempt.'—*Shakespeare.*

'MAMMA is engaged just at present,' Evelyn said, as she made a circuit of the room and straightened an antimacassar here and there; 'but I do not think she will be long.'

'Oh, it is quite right,' said Rex lightly; 'but the truth is I came across chiefly to have a little chat with you.'

'With me?' she questioned, raising her eyebrows slightly.

'Why not?' he asked.

'Oh, I know of no reason at all,' she said, with a little laugh. 'Only you have not favoured us with much of your company of late.'

'That is true,' he answered a little bit uneasily. 'But I have often wanted to come, all the same.'

'Are you always so very busy, then?' she asked a little bit gravely.

'No, not always,' he answered. 'While you were away in Scotland I had little or nothing to do, and had you been at home I should probably have worn out my welcome.'

'I don't think you need entertain any fears on that score,' she said, with a slight blush. 'You know you are always welcome at Beechlawn.'

'Thank you, Evelyn,' and then he suddenly relapsed into silence. He wanted to say more, and yet, somehow, the words would not come. He felt every moment as if his task were growing more and more difficult. She seemed so utterly unsuspicious that he shrank from shocking her with his avowal. Besides, she sat so far away from him, that it seemed almost ridiculous to try to make love across a room. And yet the precious opportunity was slipping away, and he did not know when he might get another.

'I hear you had a splendid audience last night,' Evelyn said at length, breaking the awkward silence.

'Yes,' he said slowly, and with seeming effort 'the place was full.'

'The people are loud in their praise of your lecture,' she said, after a little hesitation.

'Indeed,' he answered.

'I should very much like to have heard it,' she went on; 'but I could not get away very well.'

You had company ?' he questioned. The words were out before he had time to consider them.

She blushed slightly and looked uncomfortable; perhaps she felt the question was a rude one. But she answered readily enough: 'No, not company exactly. Mr. Stuart Leslie was here, that was all.'

'Oh, indeed,' he said shortly; 'I saw him with you also the night before last:' he was feeling desperate, so he spoke hurriedly and incautiously.

'Yes, he was with me the evening before last,' she answered, with a touch of hauteur in her tone.

Rex bit his lip: he felt that he was not advancing his cause in the least; if anything, he was retarding it.

'I meant to have run across the evening before last,' he said hurriedly; 'but I feared I might be intruding.'

'Which, under the circumstances, was considerate of you,' she answered, with mild sarcasm; for she could not help feeling that he had taken up the position of censor, and she would let him see that she resented it.

'Come now, Evelyn,' he said, with a little laugh, while he shifted uneasily in his chair; 'don't let us misunderstand each other.'

'I should be sorry to be misunderstood, and especially by you,' she said, with a ring of sincerity in her voice.

Rex's face brightened for a moment, and then

fell. What did she mean, he wondered. Did she
wish him to understand that Stuart Leslie had a
perfect right to be in her company, or did she wish
him to understand that their meeting was purely
an accident ?

'I have always made a confidante of you, Evelyn,'
he said at length ; 'you have seemed like a sister
to me nearly ever since I can remember.'

'Yes, I know,' she answered, her eyes brightening ; 'and I hope you will not depose me, or ever
think of me in any other light.'

Was she warning him off dangerous ground ?
He bit his lip again, while a puzzled expression
came into his eyes. She was certainly not giving
him any encouragement. Indeed, he began to fear
she guessed his mission and was trying to prevent
his avowal. But he was resolved not to be put
off with mere hints. He would know the truth if
possible.

'There is no fear of my deposing you,' he said at
length ; 'no one else can ever take your place.'

'Not even Julia ?' she said with a laugh.

'Not even Julia,' he said gravely ; and he drew
his chair closer to hers. 'But I have discovered
lately, Evelyn, that brotherly regard may grow into
something very different.'

Her eyes fell, and all the colour went in a moment
from her face.

'I have come to-night on purpose to tell you,' he
began, 'that you are——'

But he did not finish the sentence. At that moment a knock came to the door, followed by the entrance of Mr. Stuart Leslie. The Vicar's son came forward with the air of a man who felt perfectly at home, and who was quite sure of his footing.

Rex bit his lip with savage energy, while Evelyn rose with a soft blush suffusing her neck and face, and went quickly forward to receive her guest.

Stuart greeted Rex with effusion. 'Glad to see you, 'pon my word,' he said. 'Had quite an ovation last night, I hear; allow me to congratulate you. Should have come myself, but was—ah—more pleasantly engaged, shall I say? ha, ha!'

Rex felt that he would like to punch his head. 'Impudent puppy!' he said to himself; 'he deserves to be throttled!' But he kept his hands tightly clenched and held his tongue. But to stay longer at Beechlawn was out of the question. He had received his answer, he thought, in unmistakable language; and the sooner he left the house the better for his own peace of mind.

Evelyn pressed him to stay longer, assuring him that her mother must be disengaged directly.

'I came to see you,' he said, as she came with him into the hall; 'to see you only. I have seen you, but to stay longer now would be to intrude.'

'Rex, you talk in riddles,' she said in pained tones.

'Do I?' he said, growing very white. 'Never

6

mind, you will understand me some day;' and
without saying 'good night' he hurriedly left her
side and a moment later the door had closed
behind him.

All the way home he walked like one in a dream.
He never remembered a single step of the way.
One thought absorbed every other—Evelyn May
was lost to him. Until far into the night he paced
his den with long and rapid strides, and when
utterly exhausted crept into bed and fell into a
heavy, dreamful slumber.

The following day was among the most wretched
he had ever experienced. All the hope had been
taken out of his work, all the brightness out of his
life. He never knew how much Evelyn May was
to him till now he had lost her. He found himself
constantly dreaming over bygone days, picturing
to himself the blissful hours they had spent together rambling over the sunlit hills or loitering in
the shady woods. He could not understand how
he had been so long in arriving at the truth that he
loved Evelyn May. It seemed to him now that he
had loved her always; that there had never been a
time when she was not more to him than anyone
else.

The day being Saturday, the bank closed at noon,
and by ten minutes past that hour he was on his
way back to Barwich. After lunch he shut himself
in his own room and tried to work on a half-finished
picture, for the day was fine and the light good;

but he gave up the attempt after a few minutes. Somehow the interest had gone out of everything, and there was no heart left in him for work.

'I had better try to walk off this restlessness,' he said to himself, throwing down his palette and brushes; 'a ramble in the plantation will do me good. Perhaps I can make a study of the trees in their autumn brown and bareness;' and, thrusting a sketch-book into his pocket, he stole quietly down the broad stairs and out of the house.

As usual he made for the paddock and climbed the fence, and was soon in the field which adjoined the wood. A few minutes' brisk walking and he had reached the stile so redolent of memories of the past. But he did not linger. Leaping lightly over it, he struck up through the wood at a brisk walk, and did not pause till he had reached the summit of the hill. Here he turned round and looked back the way he had come, then struck off at right angles across the carpet of yellow leaves.

The afternoon was wonderfully still. The trees stood up motionless and bare, the delicate tracery of their branches standing out in clear relief against a pale-blue sky. On the leaf-covered sward the sunlight lay in faint yellow patches ; the wind was hushed and still.

Rex's footsteps crunching on the yellow leaves startled the squirrels here and there, and once a weazel went scuttering across his path, but no other sounds awoke the silent depths of the wood.

A few minutes' brisk walking and he had reached the boundary where the ground fell away suddenly into the valley below. There had been a small landslip some years previously, and a rail fence had been carried round the edge of the declivity, mainly for the protection of cattle.

Against this rail Rex planted himself and turned his face to the wood. Several magnificent elms grew near the spot, and he pulled his sketch-book out of his pocket and began to make a drawing of one of the trees.

Suddenly, and without warning, the rail gave way beneath his weight, and he fell backward and headlong down the slope. The collapse of the rotten rail was so sudden that he had no time to save himself or even to clutch at a tree-root in his fall.

In a moment he lay doubled up and almost hidden in the mass of brambles and bracken that covered the débris at the foot of the slope; his right leg was bent under him, the knee dislocated, his body tightly wedged between two large splinters of rock.

For a moment he lay motionless, stunned and half unconscious; but the pain from his knee quickly restored his faculties, and he made a frantic effort to rise; but he might as well have attempted to root up the tree he had been trying to sketch.

'Good heavens!' he moaned, 'must I lie here and die?' and he struggled again to free himself; but in vain. He was as helpless as if his hands and feet had been locked in steel.

'Oh, this is cruel!' he moaned bitterly. 'I shall die like a rat in a hole unless someone comes to my rescue; but who is likely to find me here?'

Then he shouted at the top of his voice: 'Help! help!' and listened eagerly for an answering call; but the only sound that greeted his ears was the occasional peck of a bird and the low murmur of the stream in the valley below.

After awhile the pain from his knee became intolerable. He almost screamed with agony. But there came no answer to his cry, nor hope of deliverance from any direction. And still the minutes sped on, and the pale autumnal sun dipped lower and lower towards the horizon. Upon his forehead a cold perspiration stood in big drops, and over his eyes a mist was gathering as though night was coming on apace. He tried again to rise, but yielded with a groan; then all grew dark and still.

CHAPTER X.

WAS IT A DREAM?

'And dreams in their development have breath,
And tears, and torture, and the touch of joy ;
They leave a weight upon our waking thoughts,
They take a weight from off our waking toils ;
They do divide our being ; they become
A portion of ourselves as of our time,
And look like heralds of eternity.'—*Byron*.

WHEN Rex recovered consciousness the afternoon was drawing rapidly to a close. The sun had disappeared in a pale-yellow haze, and all over the valley and up the hillsides a gray mist was rising, saturating everything with its moisture, and creeping lazily before the faint evening breeze. There was, however, no mist over his mind or memory. The events of the afternoon came back to him in a moment vivid and clear. And yet he had a feeling as though something had happened of which he had no exact knowledge. Between that first complete loss of consciousness and now there had been a brief space when his mind was not altogether a blank. Either he had had a dream or someone had come to him. He drew his hand slowly across his eyes and tried to recall the circumstance.

Everything else was clear enough to him. The ramble in the wood, the pencil strokes on his sketch-book, the sudden giving way of the rail, the fall among the brambles and stones, the frantic efforts he made to raise himself, the despairing calls for help, the numbness that at length crept over him and then oblivion. Up to that point everything was clear to him—there was no mist upon his memory, no shadow upon his brain.

But after that? Between that swoon and the present awakening something had happened. Was it a dream, he wondered? If so it was strangely like reality. He thought he lay there jammed between the rocks, wondering in a confused kind of way what had happened to him; that suddenly there fell upon his ears the sound of footsteps accompanied by the noise of falling stones, as some-one clambered hurriedly down the steep slope; that a moment later a voice sweet as music fell upon his ear—' Rex, Rex, what is the matter?' then a soft hand was laid upon his brow, and—and—surely it must be a dream—warm lips were pressed upon his own. He thought he struggled again to raise him-self and speak, and that gentle hands were placed under his head, and an effort made to lift him out of his uncomfortable position—then all became a blank once more.

'It must be all a dream,' he reflected; 'a sweet, beautiful dream; but nothing more than that. If Evelyn had found me here she would have stayed with me, even though she loves another.'

And a spasm of pain swept over his handsome face. 'Yes, she would not have left me,' he went on; 'but stay——' and he reached out his hands, then turned his head and looked eagerly round him.

'I have either been moved or I have moved myself,' he said with a gasp. 'The splinter of rock that was on my right has been rolled away. Is it possible that in a sudden accession of strength I could have pushed it from me unconsciously? I hardly think so; and yet would she have the power?' and he closed his eyes again and tried to think.

'One thing is certain,' he went on, after a pause: 'I am not lying in the frightfully uncomfortable position I was in at first;' and he made an effort to sit up; but the pain from his knee cut short the attempt, and he lay back again with a groan.

The more he reflected, however, the more he became convinced that someone had discovered him. But was that someone Evelyn? And if Evelyn, could it be really true that she had pressed her warm lips upon his own, and spoken words that fell with a sound of strange endearment upon his ears? If he could only think so life would become beautiful again and labour a joy. But the hope was too sweet to be cherished. Evelyn May was not for him.

At this point his reflections were cut short by the sound of voices in the wood above him, and a moment or two later half a dozen faces appeared at the edge of the slope. Then a voice, which he quickly recognised as Evelyn's, came from a little distance away.

'That is the place. He lies just below among the bracken and brambles.'

Rex's heart gave a great bound. His dream, if not wholly, was partly true. Evelyn had come to him, and, finding herself powerless to aid, had gone off into the town for help, and now she had come back again to show the way.

'Oh, Evelyn, Evelyn,' he murmured, and his eyes grew moist at the thought, 'I owe my life to you.'

What followed after that he could never very distinctly remember. There was a confused murmur of voices and scramble of feet, a feeling as though he was being torn to pieces by giant hands, and then a period of sweet forgetfulness. Then came a faint memory of being on the march, and a horribly confused idea that he was lying in his coffin and that this was his funeral; then once more oblivion.

When he opened his eyes again it was broad day. The morning sun was shining brightly into his room, and under the eaves the sparrows were chirping feebly. By his bedside stood Dr. Moffat, looking careworn and anxious.

'Hullo, doctor!' he said cheerfully, 'what's up?'

In a moment the doctor's face lit up with a broad smile.

'I'm up,' he said; 'yes, I'm up—been up all night, in fact.' And he laughed quietly at his own joke.

It was Rex's turn to be serious now. He did not need the doctor to tell him he was ill; he ached all over, and was as helpless as a child.

'I don't think I'm very well, doctor,' he said at length, bringing out the words slowly and with evident effort.

'No, you are not very well,' said the doctor, 'not very well; but you must keep quiet and not excite yourself. You've had a slight accident, you know; but don't worry yourself about it—it might have been worse—yes, yes, it might have been worse.'

'Oh yes, I remember,' he said slowly and with knitted brows. 'I was leaning against the railing above the landslip trying to sketch a tree. I like to see trees properly drawn, doctor.'

'Yes, yes, but never mind that now; I know all about it. Your business now is to get better—to get better.'

'I think trees have a distinct individuality as well as human faces,' went on Rex, as though he did not heed the doctor's words.

'Yes, yes, very likely; but don't trouble about trees now,' persisted the doctor.

'I fear I've lost my sketch-book, though,' Rex went on, with provoking pertinacity; 'but perhaps she found it—I wonder if she did.' His voice died away into a whisper, while a smile that was full of hope stole over his face.

He did not attempt to speak again, and after a few minutes Dr. Moffat quietly left the room. Later in the day a trained nurse arrived from Liverpool, and then began long weeks of weariness and pain.

Mr. Brown came to see him every three or four days, but he made his visits as brief as possible; the young man and the old had nothing in common, and neither desired the other's company. When Jonas did call, he always seemed preoccupied and ill at ease.

Ever since his marriage with Mrs. Rudd he had grown steadily more irritable and more reckless. The old habit of carefulness had almost entirely disappeared. Under his wife's influence he had become, to all appearance at least, utterly indifferent as to what was spent or what was saved. There were no more heated discussions about carefulness and economy. The servants, in their terse way, said 'everything at Elmwood was high and go,' extravagance was the order of the day.

Mrs. Brown and the two J.'s were in a chronic state of high spirits. They entertained to their hearts' content, and 'managed' Elmwood in their own way, and Mr. Brown into the bargain.

Rex saw nothing of either Mrs. Brown or her daughters. Sometimes a polite inquiry would be sent—'Mrs. Brown's respects, and she wishes to know how Master Rex is to-day'—but she never condescended to visit him herself.

Rex was not at all sorry. Yet occasionally a feeling of intense loneliness stole over him; he seemed without a relation in the world, and his home at present was to him but a better sort of hospital.

Dr. Moffat was kind, so was the nurse; but no hand of love was ever laid upon his brow, no soft caress lightened the burden of his pain. But for thoughts of Evelyn he would have grown melancholy. She, to his imagination, was ever present, and day by day he lay with closed eyes dreaming of her.

Sometimes he chided himself for his folly—said that he was preparing for himself a bitter awakening; but all the same she filled his heart, and in the main he was content to think of her alone.

So the tedious days and weeks dragged slowly on. He tried his best to be patient, but it was a difficult task. How his heart hungered in those long days for a sight of Evelyn May ! How he kept wondering whether or no she cared for him except as a friend !

Then, too, he worried about his class at the Mechanics' Institute, and chafed and fretted because he could not carry on the work he had sketched out for himself. Constantly he kept saying to himself, ' I ought to be patient,' and ' It's a foolish business to cry over spilled milk ;' but with all his

philosophy he got to be very impatient, and re-
tarded his recovery thereby. Yet events were
ripening all the while, though he had no hand in
their shaping. He little dreamed that the day was
so near when he would ask the question that lay so
heavy upon his heart, and when he would get his
answer.

CHAPTER XI.

LOVE SPEAKS OUT.

'It is the most reasonable thing in nature.
What can we do but love ?   It is our cup.
Love is the cross and passion of the heart,
Its end—its errand.'—*P. J. Bailey.*

IT wanted but a fortnight to Christmas. The day
was Wednesday, the hour three o'clock in the afternoon.   Rex for the third time had managed to
hobble downstairs, and was now seated deep in an
easy-chair in the drawing-room, staring alternately
into the fire and through the open windows upon
the wintry scene outside.

Half an hour before someone had come into the
house, and in the murmur of voices in the hall he
thought he detected the low tones of Evelyn May.
He could not be certain, and, indeed, he had to
admit to himself that the chances were it was not
Evelyn. She was not in the habit of visiting at
Elmwood ; there was no affinity between the dressy
Misses Rudd and the gentle, sweet-voiced Quaker

maiden ; and Evelyn was too sincere to make a pretence of affection where none existed.

Still, the bare possibility of Evelyn being in the house filled Rex with an indescribable unrest.

'I wonder if it be she,' he kept saying to himself; 'and if it be, I wonder if she will come and see me. And why not? We have known each other from being children, and she is not of the kind that stand much upon ceremony. Oh, what an age it seems since I saw her last! I would give almost anything for one glimpse of her sweet, pure face!' And he turned from the wintry scene he had been contemplating, and began to stare into the fire.

Suddenly his heart gave a great bound as a knock fell on the door.

'Come in,' he said, with something like a gasp.

A moment later the door opened, and, turning his head, he saw Julia with her hand still on the door-knob.

'Miss May has called to see you, Rex;' and with that announcement she made way for Evelyn and retreated, closing the door behind her.

Rex started to his feet in a moment, and stood holding by his chair while Evelyn slowly advanced to greet him. She seemed a little shyer than was her wont, but perhaps she felt that the circumstances were peculiar, or perhaps—but no, we will not suggest a reason.

'This is kind of you, Evelyn,' he said, as he stretched out his hand; and the next moment his heart thrilled as the fair, soft hand pressed his own.

'I am so glad, Rex, to see you downstairs again,' Evelyn said, with just a faint suggestion of a blush upon her neck and face ; 'you have been a prisoner a long time.'

'It has seemed a long time to me,' he answered. 'I have grown to be very impatient.'

'I do not wonder,' she said. 'We have counted the days since you were at our house.'

'I shall be heartily thankful when I am able to come again,' he said quickly.

'Not more thankful than we shall be to see you,' she answered ; then turned her head quickly to hide a blush that suddenly mounted to her face.

'I am well enough in myself,' he said, after a pause ; 'but these sprained muscles seem to require a lot of rest and coaxing;' and he tapped his knee playfully.

'It seems funny to see you with a crutch by your chair,' she said, after a pause. 'I hope you will be able to do without it soon.'

'I am afraid I shall have to use it for some time yet,' he replied ; 'but I intend trying to get out of doors in a day or two.'

'You should go for a drive ; I am sure the fresh air would do you lots of good.'

'But it's very cold, isn't it ?' he questioned.

'Yes, it's cold ; but with plenty of wraps you will take no harm.'

'I do not know,' he said dubiously; 'I think I shall have to hobble about a bit first.'

'And when you are able,' she said, with a laugh, 'you must hobble to Beechlawn. Now I must be going. I am so glad you are able to get downstairs again.'

'Nay, do not go yet,' he said, rising again to his feet. 'Please wait a few moments longer; I have so many things I want to say to you.'

'To me?' she questioned.

'Yes, to you, Evelyn. Why not?' And he sat down again.

'Oh, I do not know,' she answered, with averted eyes. 'You used to tell me most things, didn't you?'

'You were my confidante in the years gone by, Evelyn,' he said gravely. 'I think we have grown shy of each other as we have grown older.'

'You see, we cannot always be children,' she said archly.

'No, I suppose not,' he said slowly, as though considering his answer. 'I almost wish we could sometimes. We keep looking forward in the hope of something better; but I shall begin to think soon that the earliest of life's stages are the pleasantest.'

'Oh no! I don't agree with you in that a little bit,' she replied quickly. 'You are looking at the gloomy side because you have been ill and a prisoner.'

'Perhaps so,' he said musingly. 'But it was not

7

of that I wished to speak to you. I wanted to thank you in the first place for saving my life.'

' Who told you, Rex ?' she said with sudden animation.

' Why, what does that matter ?' he answered with a smile. ' It's the truth, isn't it ?'

' I believe I was the first to discover you ; but there is no merit in that.'

' Did you hear me call ?' he asked, eager to prolong the interview, and to have all the story from her lips.

' I heard a moan,' she said, ' several moans, in fact. I was returning from Thorbrig, where I had been visiting my old people ; and, to tell you the truth, I was dreadfully frightened. I thought a murder had been committed, or something almost equally terrible.'

' And yet you did not run away, Evelyn.'

' I believe I started to run,' she answered with a blush ; ' but it seemed such a cowardly thing, and in broad day too, that I stook stock-still for several seconds, and then another moan from you decided me.'

' And you came straight to the spot ?' he questioned.

' Quite straight,' she answered ; ' and when I saw the broken rail I guessed in a moment what had happened.'

' And then you rushed off to Barwich for help,' he said, looking at her steadily.

'I got help as soon as I could,' she answered, looking uneasy; 'there was nothing else I could do.'

'But you tried yourself to help me first,' he said.

'I could do nothing for you; you lay like one dead. Indeed, at first I thought you were dead.'

'And yet I heard you come, Evelyn.'

'Heard me!' she said, growing suddenly pale.

'For a long time I lay unconscious,' he replied. 'And then it seemed as though I had a dream. Someone came to me. I heard the noise of falling pebbles as someone clambered down the slope.'

'And what else?' she asked quickly, growing, if possible, paler than before.

'Ah, Evelyn, that is what I have tried to recall over and over again. I thought I heard your voice saying, "Rex, what is the matter?" I tried to move, to speak, then all became a blank again.'

Evelyn drew a sigh of relief.

'Yes, I did come to you,' she said after a pause; 'but all that I could do was to get you into a little more comfortable position.'

'But for you I should have died,' he said slowly.

'It has been a pleasure to me to have rendered you any service,' she answered with averted eyes.

'I have only one regret,' he said.

'And that?'

'That the life was not better worth the saving.'

'Oh, Rex——' she began.

'Nay, do not answer me,' he went on, 'for I have much more I want to say to you. I have

7—2

hoped a great deal during the last month or two —ay, and despaired a great deal also. But I will not trouble you with the one or the other till you have answered me a single question. I have no right to ask it, perhaps, but I cannot help myself. The question is this: Are you engaged to Stuart Leslie?'

In a moment she was on her feet; but she did not get angry; for a second or two she looked at him steadily, then burst into a low peal of laughter.

'Why, Rex,' she said, 'what can have led you to ask such a question?' ·

'I saw you together,' he muttered.

'Well, you and I have been together often,' she answered with a laugh.

'Then he is not your lover?' he questioned with a sigh of relief.

'Of course he is not,' she answered.

'Then I will speak,' he said passionately. 'Nay, Evelyn, you shall not go till you have heard me. You must have guessed by this how I love you. I came to tell you the last time I was at your house. I should have told you, only he came and prevented me. I loved you then—no words can tell how much—but since you saved my life I think my love has increased a hundredfold.'

He had risen to his feet and taken both her hands in his. She did not attempt to draw them away, and that gave him courage to proceed. Her

"I only ask you to give me a word of hope."

eyes were bent upon the floor, he saw her lips tremble.

' Oh, Evelyn,' he went on, ' you have become all the world to me, and more than all the world. But for the hope of winning you, I should wish you had left me alone to die. I do not ask you to say you love me now. I only ask you to give me a word of hope—to say you are not altogether indifferent to me.'

' Oh, Rex,' she said, suddenly raising her eyes to his, ' how can I be indifferent to you ?'

' Then you do care just a little ?' he said, his heart giving a great throb of joy.

' I care a great deal,' she answered with beautiful candour ; ' I have always cared for you.'

' My darling !' he murmured ; the next moment her beautiful head rested upon his shoulder, and he was covering her shining hair with passionate kisses.

How long they stood thus neither of them knew, but Evelyn drew herself away at length, and said, with a blush, ' Oh, Rex, what will people think ?'

' That I am the luckiest fellow on earth,' he answered, laughing.

' Nay, no flattery, please,' she said, placing her hand upon his mouth ; and for answer he caught her in his arms and kissed her.

Then they grew serious again, while she sat on the arm of his chair, her hand firmly clasped in his, and for the best part of an hour they talked of the

past and of the future. They had so much to say
to each other, so many experiences to relate, so
many plans to discuss.

Oh, those first moments of courtship! Is there
bliss on earth half so sweet ? The wintry day died
swiftly over the hills, but they did not heed the
gathering darkness. The two J.'s came more than
once to the drawing-room door and severely com-
mented upon the young people's conduct. But
Rex and Evelyn were blissfully indifferent.

At length, however, the servant came to light the
lamp, and then Evelyn, with many blushes, rushed
away, and Rex was left to his dreams.

CHAPTER XII.

LOVE AND DUTY.

For she hath lived with heart and soul alive
  To all that makes life beautiful and fair ;
Sweet thoughts, like honey bees, have made their hive
  Of her soft bosom cell, and cluster there.'—*Welby.*

THE next three months of his life, Rex looked back
upon in after-years as upon a beautiful dream—a
dream too sweet to last, too blissful to end in anything but an abrupt and painful awakening. Yet
he never regretted having had the dream. It was
something to be cherished in the memory, to be
dreamed over again a thousand times. For a little
space his life had been enriched, had been made
beautiful with peace and hope and a strong, pure
love. In his desert march he had lighted upon a
green oasis, where palm-trees grew and wells over-
flowed their banks, and for three happy months
and more he had lain in the grateful shadow of the
trees, listening to the music of the winds and the
rippling of the streams. He had known no care in

that happy time. He thought the desert way was ended, that he had found his paradise, and that for the rest of life's journey Love would light the way, and loneliness he would know no more.

Then came the rude awakening. He was out in the desert again, and alone. The green oasis had vanished, all the joy had gone out of his heart, and before him was a dark and lonely way, leading he knew not whither.

Rex himself could have filled a volume with the story of those three months. Every day brought some new pleasure as well as some pleasant duty. He recovered his strength in an incredibly short space of time, and by Christmas Eve was able to undertake the short journey to Beechlawn, where he received a welcome that would have satisfied the most exacting lover, and where his artistic talent was at once brought into requisition in decorating the rooms.

He was still too lame to do any climbing, but he could 'boss the rest,' as he tersely put it. Several London cousins had come down to spend Christmas with the Mays, girls full of fun and mischief, who made no end of sport over Rex's crutch, but were delightful girls all the same.

Rex felt a little bit shy at first, but in five minutes he was quite at home with them, and was able to return their banter with interest. Mrs. May received him with a motherly kiss, and gave him her blessing.

'You have always seemed like my boy, Rex,' she
said; 'now you are to be my son indeed.'

'And you are to be my mother,' he replied,
kissing her yet unwrinkled forehead.

'Nothing could have pleased me better, Rex,' she
went on. 'I have known you since you were a baby,
and I am not afraid to trust my little girl's happiness with you.'

Rex's eyes filled. 'I will do my best to make her
happy,' he said after a pause; 'for she is dearer to
me than my life.'

'I know it, Rex, and so I have not had a
moment's misgiving from the first. But here comes
the young puss, so I will run away, for I suppose
you will want to be together.'

Of course they wanted to be together, though
neither said so. Yet Evelyn was never unmindful
of the claims of her guests, nor would Rex selfishly
monopolize all her time. A blissful five minutes of
billing and cooing, and then they marched off into
the drawing-room, Rex leaning heavily on Evelyn's
shoulder.

'It's worth being lame to have such a crutch,' he
said playfully, and for answer she gave him one of
her happy smiles.

In the drawing-room he appropriated a big chair
in the centre of the room, from which point of
vantage he directed operations.

Of course Evelyn found an excuse for coming
near him every few minutes. The arm of his chair

seemed a capital point for studying effects, as well
as a convenient seat, while he—happy fellow!—
seemed always more prolific in suggestions when
she was near him than at any other time.

What a blissful evening that was! How full of
hope and promise! No shadow of coming events fell
upon their lives; no foreboding was in their hearts.
They had only one regret, and that was that the
evening came to an end so soon.

'Never mind, Rex,' Evelyn said, when they parted
at the door, and he was complaining of the shortness
of the evening; 'we shall meet again to-morrow.'

So the days followed each other in blissful suc-
cession. Nearly every evening he found his way
to Beechlawn, and Evelyn, with a glad light in her
eyes, was always on the look-out for his coming.

The news of their engagement was received as a
matter of course. Everybody said that no two
young people could be better fitted for each other.
Everybody but Stuart Leslie, who bit his lip and
said nothing.

Jonas Brown received the announcement with
perfect indifference. Indeed, it is to be questioned
if he quite understood what it meant. He muttered
some commonplace to the effect that 'he thought
Rex would suit the gal very well,' and then the
subject ended. Mrs. Brown and the two J.'s pro-
fessed to be delighted.

'We shall get him off our hands now,' Mrs.
Brown said, with a bland smile.

' And a very good riddance,' remarked Julia.

' I suppose pa will have to make him partner,' said Joyce.

' Or an allowance,' suggested Julia.

' Trust that to me,' said Mrs. Brown, with a toss of her stately head. ' I think I know my position.'

' It's wonderful how you have managed pa,' said Joyce, with a laugh. ' He never flares up now.'

' He knows better,' Mrs. Brown remarked — a statement which contained a measure of truth, but which was not the whole truth.

Rex saw with pain the change that had come over the man he called his father. He was no longer the careful, cautious, far-seeing man he used to be. On the contrary, he had become indifferent; nay more, in some things, he was reckless and extravagant. There was a time when wine was a luxury he rarely allowed himself; now it was evident to everyone that he was taking far more than was good for him, and under its influence he often did very foolish things. But how to check him and lead him back to better ways was a problem Rex tried in vain to solve.

With the beginning of the new year Rex took up his lectures again at the Mechanics' Institute, and further enlarged the scope of his labour by conducting a Bible-class on Sunday afternoons. This was in large measure forced upon him. He found that many of his young men were growing, or had grown, sceptical in relation to religious matters, and were disposed sometimes to speak slightingly of the Bible. This Rex could not tolerate, and yet purely religious teaching did not come within the scope of his week-evening lectures.

'I don't know what to do,' he said to Evelyn one evening, for he confided all his plans to her now, and sought her advice in almost everything. 'I have often read passages and chapters out of the Bible when I wanted to illustrate some particular subject. But evidently something more definite is required if some of them are to be saved from infidelity.'

'Why not have a Bible-class on Sunday afternoons?' she said. 'I am sure a great many of them would come.'

'Are you serious, Evelyn?' he questioned, looking at her with loving eyes.

'Quite serious, Rex.'

'I don't know,' he mused; 'I have done my best to try to persuade them to go to church or chapel, but they seem to have no inclination in that direction.'

'And yet they flock to hear Mr. Wilshaw, the infidel lecturer, when he comes.'

'Yes, that is what grieves me.'

'Then, Rex, you ought to supply an antidote to the poison. I am sure you could if you tried—they all respect you so much.'

'Yes, they respect me, I know. But to set myself up as a teacher when I so need to be taught seems almost absurd.'

'Nay, Rex, you have known the Bible from a child, and what you don't know you can learn.'

'Well, then, I have nearly everything to learn,' he said with a laugh.

'No, no!' she replied. 'You do yourself an injustice. Your duty lies in that direction, and if you do your best, God will help you.'

'Will you come and keep me in countenance if I make the attempt?' he questioned after a long pause.

'Yes, Rex, I will even do that,' she said, with a beautiful light shining in her eyes.

'Then I will make the attempt, Evelyn; and may God help me!'

So it came about that Rex hired a room for his Sunday Bible-class; and, as Evelyn prophesied, the young men rallied round him in a way that was almost an astonishment to him. Many came out of curiosity at first, others to air their doubts, some to oppose.

But Rex had the happy knack of making every subject interesting. No class could be dull while he was at the head. But apart from his skill as a teacher, the theme itself was so majestic, so full of interest, so responsive to the needs of the human heart, that the attention of his young men was easily caught and easily kept. Many of them had never made any real attempt to read the Bible before, and were surprised at its wonderful charm. Its rich majestic English, its glowing imagery, its hoary traditions, its glimpses of an unseen life, its championship of the right and the true, its denunciations of impurity and falsehood and oppression, its response to the heart's deepest longings, its revolation of the unchanging love of God, all tended to check irreverence, and to awaken an interest that would outlive the hour.

Rex did not puzzle himself or them over doctrinal subtilties. He left the exposition of creeds to the clergy. His business was to apply the ethics of the New Testament to the every-day life of his young men. He made an earnest effort to teach them to be pure and honest and truthful, to inculcate a love of virtue and honour and chivalry; nor was the effort a vain one.

In Evelyn he found a splendid helper. She entered into his plans with a zest and enthusiasm that were quite ususual with her. She seemed to have found a new interest in life, and all the future was bright with hope.

Oh, the bliss of those months! She still visited her poor at Thorbrig; but she had no longer to return alone, and the way was always too short which before had seemed so long. But events were ripening rapidly, and the trouble which was surely coming could not be much longer delayed.

CHAPTER XIII.

THE SECRET OUT.

'Let me clasp again your fingers :
  There—I press them to my lips ;
Mine are thin with all this watching.
How Time's sand too glibly slips !
Mine were warmer when my fancies
Felt the fever's dire eclipse.'—*Kent.*

IT was near the end of March. The day had been
bright and fine, though the wind still lingered in
the east, and the buds and flowers, in spite of the
sunshine, held back waiting for warmer weather.
Rex was on his way to Beechlawn, but being before
his time, he walked with slower steps than usual.
In front of him, and walking even more slowly
than himself, was a woman ; evidently she was
waiting for something or someone, and, like himself, was whiling time away. Rex slackened his
pace, but he still gained upon her. She seemed to
be scarcely moving at all. At length she stood
still and turned half round, as though something
on the opposite side of the road had attracted her
attention.

Rex felt his curiosity aroused. Who was she? Why did she linger? What did she want? Was she waiting for him? Something in her appearance, too, attracted his attention. The style and material of her attire did not harmonize. Her dress was of common stuff, and yet it was well and fashionably made. Her mantle was thin enough for summer wear, but neat and well fitting. Evidently she was someone in reduced circumstances. She knew *how* to dress, but had not the means to purchase what she needed.

As Rex got nearer, he noticed that her face did not lack refinement, though it seemed hardened with suffering and care. There was a dignity, too, in her carriage and bearing that was not without its influence upon him.

Rex was on the other side of the road, but she came across as he drew near, and stopped in front of him.

'You are Rex Brown,' she said with a gasp. Rex looked at her for a moment without replying. He was puzzled at her very evident agitation.

'That is my name,' he said, 'but you have——'

'I hope you will pardon my speaking to you,' she interrupted, bringing out the words in jerks; 'but I knew you in a moment, though I have not seen you for many years. Oh, so many and such long weary years; but I could keep away no longer.'

'Excuse me,' said Rex, with a puzzled look on his handsome face, 'but I do not understand.'

'No; of course you do not,' she replied, placing her hand on her side. 'And you will think me very rude. But if you will only hear me out.' The last words were in very pleading tones.

'If you will be brief, I shall be glad to hear what you have to say,' Rex replied in as kindly tones as possible.

'Oh, I know you will be impatient, for you are going to Beechlawn. But I have a claim upon you as well as Evelyn May.'

'What do you know of Evelyn May, and who are you?' he demanded, starting back a pace or two.

'Oh, please don't be angry,' she said, her eyes filling. 'It is so hard to say what I have come to say, and yet I am driven to it.'

'Then say on,' he said sternly.

'Nay, do not speak to me like that,' she said, with a sudden hardening of the face; 'for I am your mother.'

Rex started as though he had been shot, then stood staring at her in speechless astonishment.

'Ah, you may well be astonished,' she continued, 'and yet it is the truth I speak. I am Jane Raynor; you have heard of me often, and how I nursed Jonas Brown's baby along with my own, and how my baby died and was buried at the banker's expense.'

'Yes,' he said, with a bewildered look in his eyes; 'I have often heard the story.'

'Ah, well' she went on, 'I told a falsehood and

8

deceived them all. It was the Squire's child that died.'

'And how am I to know that you are not telling a falsehood now, and trying to deceive me?' he demanded.

'Jonas Brown's baby had a birth-mark; Dr. Moffat will describe it to you. If you are his son, you will have the mark.'

Rex bit his lip and looked at her in silence. He knew he had no mark upon him. Moreover, he had a conviction that she was telling the truth. A terrible truth it was, but the truth, nevertheless.

'And why, having kept the secret all these years, have you come now to wreck my life?' he asked at length, in a voice which he tried in vain to steady.

'To wreck your life? No!' she said eagerly. 'Have I not suffered for years for your sake, that you might be educated and brought up like a gentleman? All I ask now is that, if you believe I am your mother, you will help me. You are rich, and we are, oh, so poor, and my husband—your father—is ill in bed.'

'But do you think I can be a party to this deception?' he demanded sternly. 'Can I call myself Rex Brown when I know it is not my name, and live at Elmwood when I know I am an interloper——'

'And why not?' she said eagerly. 'You are wronging no one. You are keeping no one out of his rights. When I gave you up I did what I thought was for the best. I give you up still. I only ask that in our poverty you will help us.'

'And you have told me this to show you have a claim upon me ?' he questioned.

'I have always hoped that you would help us,' she said.

'But you have not calculated on my refusal to be a party to such deception.'

'I never dreamed for a moment you would wish it otherwise,' she said. 'Would you give up all your prospects in life, give up the girl you are going to marry, and hold up your own mother to contempt and obloquy ?'

'I never thought of you,' he said, with downcast eyes.

'I was sorely tried,' she went on after a long pause, and with a look in her eyes which clearly betokened that her thoughts were back in the past. 'We were very poor, and I had to decide so quickly. It nearly broke my heart to give you up, but it seemed the best—the best for poor Mrs. Brown, whose life was wrapped up in her baby; the best for us, for we could barely feed the mouths we had ; and the best for you, for you would be sure of a home and plenty.'

'The best for me,' he said passionately. 'Oh, heaven, I know not.'

'Perhaps I ought not to have told you,' she said, wringing her hands. 'And yet how could I claim

help of you unless you know; and help we must
have or starve.'

'I would have helped you anyhow,' he said, with
eyes still bent upon the ground. 'And perhaps,
after all, it is best I should know.'

'No harm need come of your knowing, anyhow,'
she said. 'And, oh, the telling has eased my
heart! The secret has been a weary burden all
these years.'

'I fear it will be a weary burden to me also,' he
answered. 'And yet it must be right that I should
know.'

'Oh, I am glad you do not think I have done
wrong in telling you.'

'I do not know where the wrong ends and the
right begins,' he said after a pause. 'But I must
have time to think.'

'I will not see you again if you wish me to keep
away,' she replied. 'If you would send us a little
help now and then, I would try to be satisfied.'

'Where are you living?' he asked abruptly.

'Down on the Welsh coast,' she said, 'in a little
fishing village called Aberfae; several other artists
are there. I think that was the attraction to my
husband. Ah me! we have sometimes wanted
bread.'

'I am very sorry,' he said slowly; 'very sorry—
I will come and see you soon. If your story is true,
it is right I should know my father.'

'Oh, but he must never know!' she said in

terrified tones. 'I could not bear that he should know I had deceived him all these years.'

Rex groaned. The situation became more and more complicated every moment. Only one thing was clear—life could never be the same again. That fatal secret changed everything. A few minutes ago he was the happiest man alive; now he was the most miserable: the terrible truth he had heard from this woman's lips had laid a burden upon him almost too great to be borne.

He took his purse out of his pocket at length, and handed it to her.

'You will find sufficient there to last you a week or two,' he said. 'And in the meanwhile I will consider what is to be done.'

'But you will promise not to divulge my secret?' she questioned eagerly. 'I have always tried to do right; and if in this thing I did wrong, I thought I was doing for the best.'

For a moment or two he looked at her steadily. And in those moments his heart unconsciously went out to her. He could not doubt, as he looked at her, that she was his mother. And if she had done wrong, she had done it for his sake, and had paid a bitter penalty for many years.

'I will not blame you,' he said pityingly; 'but I cannot make any such promise as you ask. You have told me the secret of your own free will. I may think it right and best to divulge it.'

'Oh, no, no; for my sake do not,' she pleaded;

'I never thought for a moment you would entertain such an idea.'

'I am of age now,' he replied, 'and must be left to decide on my own course of action.'

'But, surely, you will not disgrace me and ruin yourself?' she answered quickly. 'Of what account would be all my suffering and scheming and waiting, if you gave up the position I placed you in? Think of it; think what you would lose. Think of the disgrace and humiliation. Think how you would turn my husband against me for practising this deception during so many years. And think, too, that nothing could possibly be gained by your telling.'

'I *will* think,' he said, turning away from her fierce and pleading eyes. 'Now go away. Can you reach Aberfae to-night?'

'Yes. Though it will be very late before I get there.'

'Then go away—you shall see me or hear from me soon. Is that enough?'

For answer, she took his hand and kissed it, then turned and walked hurriedly away.

CHAPTER XIV.

UNCERTAINTY.

'That shadowy consciousness will steal
O'er every scene of fond desire,
Linger in laughter's gayest peal,
And close each cadence of the lyre.'
Earl of Carlisle.

EVELYN could not understand her lover that
evening, he was so unlike his usual self. When at
his best, Rex was a splendid conversationalist—
bright, witty, sparkling. On most evenings he had
some bit of news to tell or plan to discuss. But
to-night he sat moody and silent, with a far-away
look in his eyes, which Evelyn was quick to notice
but slow to understand. Rex did his best to
appear as usual, but the attempt was a sorry
failure. Try as he would, the words he had heard
that evening haunted him and would not leave
him for a single moment, while ever before him
was that pale, careworn face, telling of long years
of longing and suffering for his sake.

Once or twice he got up from his chair and

shook himself, as though he would banish from his memory some painful dream.

At length Evelyn could keep silent no longer. 'What *is* the matter with you, Rex?' she said, with a touch of anxiety in her tone.

He started and coloured slightly, then answered slowly: 'I hardly know, Evelyn; I am scarcely myself to-night.'

She had been sitting at the piano, but she got up from her seat and came and stood by his chair, and placed her soft white hand upon his forehead.

'Oh, Rex,' she said, 'you are quite hot and feverish. I hope you are not going to be ill.'

'I hope not,' he answered absently; but he shivered under her touch as though he had been smitten with ague.

'I am sure you are quite ill,' she said quickly. 'Oh, Rex, why did you not say so? Let me call mother.'

'No, no,' he replied, colouring more deeply than before. 'I shall be all right again soon. Don't alarm yourself, Evelyn.'

'How can I help being alarmed, Rex, when I see you so poorly?'

'My darling,' he whispered, while the tears welled up suddenly into his eyes.

She laid her soft cheek against his hot forehead for answer, while her hand sought his and nestled in its firm grasp.

For several minutes they remained thus—minutes

which should have been to Rex full of purest bliss, but which were in reality crowded with an unspeakable pain. He felt like a hypocrite and a liar. He was making love to this beautiful girl under false pretences. He had no right to be in this house at all—no right to be in the town. He was not Rex Brown, the banker's son, and the heir of Elmwood. He was the son of an unknown painter, a child of poverty and toil.

And over his neck and face swept hot blushes of pain and shame and humiliation. Should he throw himself at Evelyn's feet and confess all? Tell her all the story he had heard that night, and then leave her if she wished it, never to see her face again?

Was it prudence that whispered, 'Say nothing yet. Wait till you are certain. You may have been deceived. Act with caution and bide your time?'

So he waited, and tried his best to quiet Evelyn's fears by assuring her that though he was a little out of sorts he was not really ill.

He left Beechlawn much earlier than usual, glad for the first time in his life to escape its warm atmosphere and to get into the open air. Out under the pale stars he felt less like a hypocrite and an impostor than when by Evelyn's side. Yet how changed the world was! That brief story to which he had listened had transformed everything. He felt, with a bitter sense of loss and pain, that life could never be again as it had been. This cruel secret was like a stone upon his heart: it seemed to chill his very blood and clog all his energies.

In the road where that strange meeting had taken place, a few hours before, he paused and looked round him. No one was near; overhead, the stars burned brightly, and in the tall bare trees the keen wind wailed dolorously.

'I wonder if it was all a dream?' he said to himself. 'Suppose I leaned there against that bank and fell asleep for a moment and dreamed it all. Such things have happened. Am I dreaming now?' And he rubbed his eyes to make sure.

The next moment he started and turned pale, as an owl flew swiftly past him, with heavy flapping wings, and vanished in the darkness.

'I believe I am growing morbid and super-stitious,' he muttered. 'I had better get home and to bed as quickly as possible.'

Then he started again. 'Home,' he said; 'I have no home. At least, not here. I am an interloper and a usurper. Oh, heavens, that I should have lived to see this day!'

It was far on into the morning before he got a wink of sleep, and even when slumber did seal his eyelids it failed to refresh him, so full was it of painful and distressing dreams. One thing, how-ever, he resolved to do before he fell asleep, and that was to consult Dr. Moffat at the earliest opportunity and ascertain the truth or falsehood of the birth-mark story. 'If the doctor says Mrs

Brown's baby had a birth-mark,' he said to himself, 'then I shall know she has spoken the truth. If, however, he knows nothing about it, then I shall know she has been deceiving me and levying blackmail.'

Yet when morning came he felt much less anxious to see the doctor. In his heart he believed the story he had heard, yet until it was confirmed by the doctor, he argued, there was room for reasonable doubt, and with this doubt he tried to satisfy his conscience.

'It would be very foolish of me,' he said to himself, over and over again, 'to accept the unconfirmed story of a strange woman. Likely enough it is a pure fabrication, intended only to get money out of me.'

Yet in his heart he felt all the while that the story was true enough. He understood now his unlikeness to Jonas Brown, and to the woman he had once called his mother. He understood also from whence came his artistic gift. He was the son of a painter, and that explained everything.

But the days sped on and he did not go near Dr. Moffat. Then he heard that the doctor had gone away for a week or two, and he drew a sigh of relief. At last there was a little respite. He could not act until he knew, and he could not know until the doctor returned, so he locked the secret in his heart, and tried to appear as usual ; but it was very difficult.

His Sunday-afternoon class tried him terribly. He had been trying for months past to inculcate a pure and noble morality; had insisted that right should be done and truth spoken regardless of consequences. Now the advice he had given seemed to stick in his throat. How easy it was to preach, how difficult it was to practise!

If the members of his class knew, he thought, how they would discount his teaching! Nay, they would even despise him, while Evelyn would spurn him from her side as an unprincipled pretender.

He felt after awhile that he was losing moral stamina and force. He was acting a part to the detriment of his moral nature. The very effort to hide his feelings, to appear to be other than he was, inflicted damage upon him which he was early conscious of.

Yet what could he do? He seemed sliding down a steep acclivity without power to restrain himself, or even to check the rate of his descent. His courage seemed to be steadily evaporating, while the more he thought of what the exposure meant, the more he shrank from confirming the truth.

Evelyn grew daily more perplexed at his demeanour. Fits of abstraction were followed by fits of almost boisterous mirth. His very effort to appear natural made him appear unnatural. Sometimes he would sit for an hour on the stretch staring into vacancy; then he would start up with a bewildered look in his eyes, and an uneasy feeling of impending danger in his heart.

Once or twice Evelyn had said to him in beseeching tones, ' Do tell me what is the matter, Rex;' but he had replied that he was all right, with such a pained look in his eyes that she forbore at length to ask any more questions, though she stored up all these things in her heart, and brooded over them in silence and with many misgivings.

As the days dragged on their slow lengths, Rex felt that his life had become a martyrdom. He began to feel that he had acted weakly and foolishly; that he should have proved the truth or falsehood of the story at the very beginning; that by delaying he was making his path increasingly difficult. Moreover, the one doubt that existed in the case was no comfort to him at all; on the contrary, it was a pain, and a source of uneasiness and unrest. He became anxious for Dr. Moffat's return, and impatient at his delay.

' I will know the truth as soon as he returns,' he said to himself; 'and if he confirms her story, why, then——'

But he left the sentence unfinished. In truth, he had not decided how he would act in such an event. He would wait till the time came. There was just a possibility the story might be a fabrication, and while that possibility existed he would decide nothing.

After an absence of ten days, Dr. Moffat returned

again to Barwich. Rex saw him driving home from the station one evening as he was hurrying to his class at the Mechanics' Institute.

'I will know the truth to-night,' he said to himself, growing very pale, and turning almost sick at the thought. 'Anything is better than this uncertainty.'

It could not be said that his address to his young men that evening was a success. It was heavy, laboured, and lacking in lucidity. Its one redeeming feature was brevity.

'I am not at all well,' he said by way of apology, 'so you must excuse a longer address to-night.'

And then, as soon as possible, he hurried away through the streets to learn the truth from the lips of the kindly old doctor.

CHAPTER XV.

'Still o'er these scenes my memory wakes,
  And fondly broods with miser's care.'
Time but the impression deeper makes,
  As streams their channels deeper wear.'
                                    Burns.

WHEN Rex returned to Elmwood an hour later he knew the worst. He had consulted Dr. Moffat ostensibly on the ground of his general health and a lingering weakness in his knee. But it was easy to drift into a talk about old times, and by a few judicious questions, skilfully put, all the truth came out.

The old doctor was growing garrulous, and nothing pleased him better than a talk about the past.

'I suppose I must be getting old,' he said; 'though in some respects I feel as young as ever— ay, as young as ever; but the sight of so many strapping young fellows about me, whom I knew as babies, makes me feel that I must be getting on;

not a very pleasant feeling, Rex, but one has to submit—has to submit.'

'Yes, I suppose so,' Rex answered slowly.

'Ah, boy, you know nothing about it—nothing about it. You have life and the world all before you, and a pleasant prospect you have; at least, I should think so if I stood in your shoes.'

'Yes, the prospect is not bad,' Rex said with a slight shrug of his shoulders.

'Not bad? I should think not. The heir of Elmwood marrying the loveliest girl for twenty miles round! Bless my soul and body, I almost envy you! What does your father say about it?'

'Not very much. He isn't much given to talking; at least, to me. You know we're not much alike.'

'Much alike, no. There isn't a single point of likeness. Though that's not much to trouble about—eh? You're like your mother.'

'But for her, people might doubt my identity!' Rex said with a laugh.

'Yes, yes; but you've always an answer in that birth-mark, Rex. Convenient things sometimes, when they don't disfigure.'

'You remember it, then?' Rex said, looking the old doctor straight in the eyes.

'Remember it? Well, rather. Little things of that sort I never forget. In some instances my memory has come in handy in such things. Let me give you a case in point.'

And the old doctor rambled away into a seemingly interminable story, which Rex had great difficulty in following; and when it was finished he rose quietly and took his departure.

Home through the quiet and almost deserted streets he walked, with slow and uncertain steps. Sometimes he felt half disposed never to enter Elmwood again. He might go away under cover of the night and lose himself in some out-of-the-way place, dropping the name he had borne so long and starting life afresh.

In time the old life might seem to him like a dream, and grow gradually more shadowy and indistinct, till he might be able to think of it without pain, and without any sense of loss.

Then the vision of Evelyn's pure and lovely face came up before him, and scattered the half-formed purpose like dust before a storm. Elmwood he might give up, and the fortune to which he was supposed to be heir; but to root the love out of his heart, and hide in silence from her who was more to him than life, that was impossible.

So he crept quietly into the house as though he had been a thief, and slowly mounted the stairs to his own room. Here he found the gas turned low, and a cheerful fire crackling in the grate. For Rex was a favourite with all the servants, and so was never neglected under any pretence.

He locked the door as soon as he got into the room, and turned up the gas, then stood for a long

9

time on the hearthrug looking round him. It was a den that any bachelor might be proud to own. Choice rugs lay on the floor, choice paintings and etchings adorned the walls, choice books filled the shelves. On tables and brackets were bits of sculpture, and bric-à-brac of all descriptions; while drawings of his own, which revealed a true artist's skill, stood on easels in different parts of the room.

Over the mantelpiece was a portrait of Evelyn, which he had only just finished, and which was, in its way, a gem in portraiture. It had been to him a labour of love, but he had thrown into it as well all his skill, and the result was satisfactory from every point of view. Indeed, it came nearer satisfying Rex — and he was hard to please — than anything he had ever done before.

As his eye fell upon one pleasant object after another he heaved a deep sigh.

'It will be hard to leave it all and go forth penniless into the world,' he muttered to himself. 'I've never been brought up to rough it, and in the struggle for existence I fear I shall cut a sorry figure—that is, if I ever make the attempt.'

Then he threw himself into a deep wicker chair and stared long and earnestly into the fire.

'I've got to the parting of the ways at last,' he said, after a long pause. 'I may as well face the situation fairly, and weigh the pros and cons. There is no longer any doubt on the question of identity. I am not Rex Brown. I am just an interloper, and have no more right in this room than any of the clerks in the bank—and never have had, for that matter. The proper thing for me to do would be to clear out as quickly as possible, strip myself of all disguise, expose the deception, and face the world like any other penniless beggar, and take my chance.'

And he ran his fingers through his hair, and stared still more earnestly into the fire.

'Well,' he said, after another pause, 'I never saw right and wrong so tangled before. Assuming it is the right thing to confess all, and leave all, what is the good that will come out of it? Will anybody be benefited? Will any wrong be redressed? Will any life or any home be made happier? Not that I can see. I may secure an easy conscience. But any other good likely or unlikely to come out of it I cannot discover.

'And now for the other side. By doing the right—if it is right—I leave Mr. Brown without a son. I wreck my own prospects in life. I give up my useful work among the young men. I destroy Evelyn's happiness and hope—for the time, at least. I disgrace my mother; turn her husband, my father, against her after all these years of wedded life—in short, create misery all round and bring good to nobody.

'How, then, can a thing be right when it produces only trouble, without any corresponding good? And how can a thing be wrong when all concerned are benefited thereby, and injustice is done to no one?'

Truly right and wrong had, to all appearance, changed places. Looking at the matter purely in the abstract, his course seemed clear enough; but when he tried to measure up the consequences, then everything became confused and uncertain. It was the old battle over again, in which his mother had been defeated more than twenty long years before. How strangely history repeats itself! How certain the harvest of our deeds. Little did Jane Raynor think when she yielded to the voice of the tempter that she was preparing a hard and cruel struggle for her son. For herself she knew there would be suffering in store, but for him she pictured only bliss.

Had she known Rex better, she would have hesitated before telling him the secret. But she did not dream it would trouble him much. She had—or thought she had—so completely satisfied herself that she had done the right thing, and that there was no wrong in it, that she naturally supposed he would look at the question in the same light.

But Rex's conscience was not so easily satisfied; and yet to the ever-recurring questions, What good will come of it? whom am I wronging? he could get no satisfactory answer.

'I know I have no right here,' he kept saying to himself; 'I know I am an interloper—ay, and an

impostor. But it is not my fault; I did not place
myself here, nor am I keeping anyone else out of
his rights. If I go away I remedy nothing. No
one will be the gainer, while I shall disgrace my
mother, ruin my own prospects, and lose Evelyn
for ever.'

And, getting up from his chair, he marched round
the room again and again, then suddenly dropped
into his chair as though exhausted. So the battle
raged hour after hour, and he seemed no nearer
the victory than at the start.

Rex was no saint, nor did he yearn for martyrdom.
He wanted to do the right if it could be accomplished
without too great a sacrifice. But he was not prepared to give up everything for a mere whim or
idea.

As the night wore away the issues seemed to
grow more and more confused, so he crept into bed
just before the morning began to pale, and soon fell
into a troubled sleep.

The next day he was still undecided, and the
day after that. He got so far as to say he was
prepared to sacrifice himself—to give up all his
own hopes and prospects. But to inflict this cruel
pain on his mother, who had already suffered so
much on his account, was what he could not bring
himself to do.

So the days sped on and lengthened into weeks
but his conscience refused to be reconciled. He
could find no peace anywhere. He imagined that

people looked suspiciously at him, that the secret
had leaked out and was being passed from lip to
lip, that people were biding their time to see if he
would behave like a man and make a clean breast
of it, and that if he did not, they would suddenly
pounce upon him and denounce him as an impostor.

He began to fear Jonas, and Mrs. Brown, and the
two J.'s. Perhaps the haughty ways and words of
the latter meant more than appeared on the
surface. Did they suspect anything? Were they
waiting only to make his humiliation more complete?

Life became a torture after awhile. He did not
crave martyrdom. But martyrdom had come to
him. Every spark of joy had gone out in darkness.
There seemed nothing left worth living for.

It was towards the end of April when the crisis
came. 'I have been a cheat long enough,' he
moaned in his misery. 'For the future I will be
myself and take my chance.'

CHAPTER XVI.

TRUTH WILL OUT.

'We'll quit the race for selfish end,
　　Where bubbles swell and break,
And dwell where peace and virtue blend,
　　And thus life's music wake.
We'll cheat no more, nor cheated be
　　By blare, or glare, or cry ;
But wash the feet, the face, and see
　　Real life with open eye.'—*W. H. Wood.*

MRS. MAY and Evelyn had been in London about
a fortnight, and expected to stay another ten or
twelve days. Rex was not at all sorry. Indeed,
he felt rather relieved than otherwise. He had
grown so suspicious of late that he was at his ease
nowhere. His evenings with Evelyn, instead of
being a joy, had become almost a torture. He
feared she would read suspicion on his very face,
and if any evening she had denounced him as an
impostor, he would not have been surprised.

He regretted now he had not told her as soon as
he knew the truth, and left his fate in her hands.
He knew well enough that she had loved him for
himself alone, and not for his name, or the estates

to which he was supposed to be heir. Had he told her then, she would probably have still remained loyal to him, and helped and encouraged him in his battle with the world.

But now he had deceived her—had raised between them an impassable barrier.

'I have made love to her,' he said, 'under false pretences. I have been a consenting party to a huge imposture. I have forfeited every right to any consideration. When she knows, she will lose all respect for me, to say nothing of love. My name will become a by-word on her lips, and she will forget me as soon as possible. That is the penalty of my own wrong. Well, so be it. To keep up the imposture longer would be a still greater penalty. The burden of this secret would kill me in a year.'

So he wrote a long letter to Evelyn and told her all.

'I have kept the secret,' he said, 'until I can keep it no longer. I feel it is driving me mad. I ought to have told you at once, but I was weak and a coward. Moreover, I shrank from giving pain to her who had suffered so much for me. How could I proclaim my mother's wrong? Nor was that all. Oh, Evelyn, I wanted to keep you, and be to you what I had always been. The thought of losing you filled me with despair. I did not see at the first that by hiding the truth I was going the only way to lose you. I see it now

when it is too late. Think of me as kindly as you
can. But you will soon forget me, and it is well
you should. You will get this letter to-morrow
morning. To-morrow morning I shall tell Mr.
Brown, and then I shall go away. Where, I know
not. My father and mother I must leave in peace.
I dare not come between them. I have made up
into a parcel all the things I have which belong to
you, and will send them to Beechlawn to-morrow.
Some of the things I should like to keep for many
reasons, but I dare not do so. Farewell, Evelyn.
Oh, how I should like to look upon your face once
more; but it may not be. But your face is graven
upon my heart; there it will remain till death shall
end the struggle.'

Having posted the letter, he stole quietly to his
room, where he remained till bedtime, putting his
things in order. He slept very little that night,
the tumult in his heart was too great; and when he
came downstairs next morning he was pale and
hollow-eyed, though the apprehensive look which
had been noticeable for several weeks past had
entirely disappeared.

It was late in the afternoon, however, before he
got the desired interview with Mr. Brown.

'Now, Rex,' said Jonas in his abrupt style,
'what's up? Want to get married right off, eh?'

And he stuck his back against the mantelpiece,
and gathered up his coat-laps on his arms.

'No, sir, I have no thoughts of getting married,'

Rex said quietly, but with a slight tremor in his voice, for in a moment there came up before his mental vision a picture of what might have been.

'No thought of gettin' married, eh?' Jonas questioned with a grunt. 'Well, p'raps you're wise. Marriage ain't all jam-tart an' cream.'

'I have made a very important discovery lately,' Rex said, without heeding Mr. Brown's remark; 'and I am taking this opportunity of communicating it to you. I ought to have done so before.'

'A discovery, eh? Something in the shape of an invention, you mean?'

'No, not an invention,' Rex went on. 'I have discovered that I am not your son.'

Jonas fairly jumped, then stared at Rex for a moment in speechless astonishment.

'Not my son?' he gasped at length, growing very red in the face and breathing hard.

'Such is the truth,' Rex said quietly.

'Heavens!' and Jonas dropped his coat-laps, while his heavy jaw worked uneasily.

'You can guess the rest, I think,' Rex said at length.

Jonas stared at him for a long time, then muttered: 'You are Raynor's child?'

'Yes.'

'Palmed off upon me when my own child died?'

'Yes.'

'An' fed, an' clothed, an' heducated all these years at my expense?'

"'Yes,' he said, 'I give her up also.'"

' Quite true.'

Jonas muttered an explotive which we will not record. The thought of the imposition angered him.

' When did you got to know this ?' he demanded.

'A month ago.'

' Who told you ?'

' My mother !'

' Bah ! does the word stick in thy throat ? Thy mother !—yes, that accounts for thy plebeian ways,' and Jonas got so red that Rex almost feared an attack of apoplexy.

For awhile the two men stood facing each other in silence. Then Jonas demanded : ' What next ?'

' I go away,' Rex said quietly. ' I have no right here. I hope I may be able to carn my living, and if in the years to come I can pay back what I have cost you, it shall be done.'

' An' you relinquish everything ?'

' Everything.'

' And the gal ! do you give her up ?'

Rex dropped his eyes for a moment while his lips quivered.

' Yes,' he said ; ' I give her up also.'

Jonas relented. Though he had never shown any strong affection for Rex, yet he could not help liking him after a fashion. He was the only son he had ever known, and the idea of being left childless, with no one to bear his name when he was dead, was not a very agreeable one.

'You need not have told me this, Rex,' he said at length.

'I did not tell you till I was absolutely sure,' was the answer.

'But why did you tell me at all ?'

'I could bear the secret no longer. I felt like a thief in the house.'

'Yes, yes. But it upsets things terrible, you see.'

'For me it does.'

'It does for everybody,' said Jonas.

'I have thought of all that,' Rex said at length— 'discussed the matter with myself till my brain has reeled. But truth will out. I could endure the imposture no longer.'

'Humph ; I b'lieve I should have endured it had I been in your place,' Jonas answered. 'It ain't a joke to give up such prospects as yours. Not that I shall leave you much—that is—well, that ain't 'ere or there. But the gal will have a pile.'

Rex remained silent, and Jonas took a turn round the room.

'Look here,' he said, at length, stopping in front of Rex ; 'I don't b'lieve in doing things all of a sudden ; you needn't go away just yet. You've lived here all your life. It ain't your fault you were palmed off on me, and I can understand the fix Raynor's wife would be in at the time ; and— and—well I might consider whether I might not——'

Then Jonas paused and looked towards the door ;

he fancied he heard a noise behind the screen. It
was not repeated, however, so he went on :

'I was saying I might consider the propriety of
adopting you or——'

'Not if I know it, Mr. Brown,' said Mrs. Brown,
advancing with dignified step.

'You here?' gasped Jonas.

'Yes, I came seeking you, and, catching some
words that interested me, I waited awhile behind
the screen.'

'And you've heard?'

'Yes, I've heard that this creature' (with a wave
of her hand towards Rex) 'is an impostor, which
I have always believed from the first. Anybody
with half an eye could see he was no son of
yours.'

'You never said so,' grunted Jonas.

'I had no proof.'

'You've no proof now.'

'He admits it himself; that is enough. And
now he goes.'

'Goes?'

'Yes! Do you think I will harbour an impostor
in my house?'

'The house is mine,' ejaculated Jonas.

Mrs. Brown stamped her foot.

'Jonas Brown, do you hear me? He goes, and
at once.'

'He cannot go to-night,' Jonas said.

'Then he goes the first thing in the morning.'

And Mrs. Brown marched out of the room to seek her daughters.

'I fear it is all up, Rex,' said Jonas.

'It's best I should go,' was the quiet answer. 'I thank you for your kindness; some day I hope I may in some measure repay you.'

So they parted. Rex was glad to remain another night, for he had a lingering hope that Evelyn might reply to his letter, in which case it would reach Elmwood by the morning's post. If she would only send him a kind message of forgiveness, he thought he could go away content. And he knew if she sent such a message it would come by return of post.

He was up early next morning, and when the letters came he scanned them eagerly, but there was no letter for him. Evelyn had not written.

In the breakfast-room he sat down to the table alone. Mr. and Mrs. Brown and the two J.'s did not come near him. He had ordered a cab for 7.45, and punctually at the time it drove up to the door.

The servants knew nothing, and he gave them no hint of what had happened. They brought his couple of portmanteaus downstairs, and gave them into the hands of 'Cabby,' then stood till he had donned his overcoat and hat.

He bowed and smiled when he went out of the door, as he always did; and they smiled and bowed in return. Then the door closed and the cab drove away.

And so the old life ended, and so began the new.

CHAPTER XVII.

A FRESH PAGE.

'Is it instinct? or some spirit
   Which protects us and controls
Every impulse we inherit,
   By some sympathy of souls?
Is it instinct? Is it nature?
   Or some freak or fault of chance,
Which our liking or disliking
   Limits to a single glance?'—*Charles Swain.*

REX turned the new page in his history without
any clear or definite idea as to the course he should
pursue. He would go to London and lose himself
among its seething millions. But what after that
was by no means clear. Perhaps Providence would
lead him, or fortune favour him, or luck give him
a new start; or perhaps—but no, he would not
anticipate failure; with a clear head and a pair of
strong hands he was not going to fail. All the
world was before him, and he meant to succeed.

He was not nearly so down-hearted as might
have been expected. In spite of the pain of leaving
the old home, there was something exhilarating in

the thought of facing the world in his own strength,
and fighting his way by his own endeavour.

Now that the secret was out, and he was no
longer driven to the necessity of acting a part, he
felt a buoyancy and a sense of relief that were some
compensation for the sacrifice he had made.

'I feel that I have done the right thing,' he said
to himself, lifting his hat and pushing his fingers
through his thick brown locks. And before he
reached the station he was actually humming to
himself Faber's well-known lines :

> 'For right is right, as God is God ;
>   And right the day must win.
> To doubt would be disloyalty ;
>   To falter would be sin.'

At the station he rushed up to the booking-office
intent on taking a ticket to London. The words
'Euston' had nearly passed his lips when he paused
suddenly. From whence came that sudden suggestion—'Go to Aberfac ?' It was as though a
voice spoke close to his ear. He looked round him
with an uneasy, apprehensive feeling. But the voice
was still echoing in his heart, 'Go to Aberfac.'

'And why not ?' he said to himself. 'I need not
make myself known. I can lose myself as well
there, perhaps, as in London. Perhaps my parents
need help. Moreover, I should like to see my
father. I will go.'

He took his ticket for Aberfac, never doubting
that again he had done the right thing. Indeed,

he began to wonder that he had never thought of it before. As the forenoon wore slowly away, and he was still far from his journey's end, he began to grow impatient. He felt like an emigrant returning to his home after a long absence. He was longing to look upon his father's face, and hear the sound of his mother's voice.

From the moment he had resolved to go to Aberfae there had sprung up in his heart a new and strange affection. The word 'father' clothed itself with a deeper meaning, and 'mother' sounded wonderfully sweet as he repeated it softly to himself.

Since that meeting in the lane a month ago, there had been a feeling of resentment in his heart against the woman who claimed to be his mother. But it had all vanished now. Perhaps this bright, sunshiny morning had driven it away. Perhaps the bracing breath of those beautiful Welsh hills had removed it. Anyhow, it was gone; and his heart began to yearn for a sight of her pale, suffering face. She had done for the best; and if she had done wrong she had paid a bitter penalty. But whatever she had done or left undone, she was his mother.

So the tender affection grew and ripened as the hours of that first of May morning passed on. It was noon when the half-empty train pulled up with a series of jerks in Aberfae Station. Rex was on the platform almost before it stopped, and, looking swiftly around him, he drew a sigh of relief. A grand sweep of hills encircling a lovely bay, on

10

either side of which bold headlands stood out in
clear relief against the shining sea. A river yonder
with a deep channel; and, clustering on its farther
bank and rising up the hillside, the gray stone
houses of the fisher folk. Such was the picture
that met his gaze. A quiet, sleepy, old-world place,
full of beauty and romance and superstition.

Leaving his portmanteaus in the cloak-room, he
marched away to the village, which was at least a
mile distant, though it looked much nearer. The
babbling river—clear from the mountains—was
crossed by a narrow but strongly-built bridge;
a sudden turn to the right and he entered the
straggling village.

Here mingled odours greeted his nostrils—coal-
tar from the boats, seaweed from the beach, and
bark from the hillside, where the fishermen were
hanging out their nets to dry, all contributed their
quota.

'Do you know where John Raynor lives?' Rex
asked of a woman who sat in her doorway nursing
a baby; but she only shook her head.

'You do not know?' he questioned.

And then she gave him to understand she could
not speak English.

The discovery gave Rex quite a shock of surprise.
He had never been in 'Welsh Wales' before, and
it seemed almost incredible that people could live
all their lives on this British isle and not speak the
English language.

Farther down the street was a group of children playing a noisy game, and jabbering and shouting at each other in a foreign tongue. Rex paused for a minute or two, then pursued his way with a look of perplexity upon his face.

At length a policeman came to his rescue. Police-constable Rees could speak a little English.

'Yes, he did know John Raynor. He wass a painter. He wass not very well. He lived——' and he took Rex by the sleeve and drew him down the street till opposite a lane leading up the hill-side. 'That iss the 'ouse,' he said, pointing with his finger.

'The white-washed cottage with a green-slate roof?' Rex questioned.

'Yes, indeed.'

A few minutes later Rex stood before the door. 'Come in!' came a feeble voice from within in response to his knock; and, lifting the door-latch, he entered.

There was no hall or passage, the door opened into the little sitting-room; and almost before he was aware he was face to face with his mother. But what a change one short month had wrought! Half sitting, half reclining in a deep easy-chair, her head supported with pillows, her wasted hands lying listless on the blanket that covered her, was Jane Raynor, gasping out the small residue of her sad and sorrowful life.

She did not recognise him for a moment, his

10—2

back was toward the light. But when he came nearer and took her wasted hand in his, she gave a low, glad cry, 'Oh, Rex, Rex!' and burst into tears.

Without a word he knelt on the floor, and laid his forehead on the arm of her chair; and then the wasted and feeble fingers strayed among his sunny locks, while grateful tears that eased her overburdened heart stole silently down her sunken cheeks.

A mother's hand upon his head touched his heart in a way he could not understand.

'I am so sorry you are ill,' he murmured at length.

'I am nearly home, Rex,' she gasped. 'And now that you have come I can die content, for God has answered my prayer.'

'Your prayer?' he questioned.

'For days and weeks I have prayed for a token of forgiveness. And your coming was the token I pleaded for. I asked Him, if I was forgiven, to let you come before I died. Now I know He has heard me.'

For answer, Rex lifted her wasted hand to his lips and kissed it.

A swift rush of tears blinded her for a moment and choked her utterance; but when she was able to speak, she said:

'You do not hate me, Rex?'

'No, mother; I love you.'

Then she began to cry again. It was more than she expected, and she was weak with much suffering.

'I thought I was doing for the best,' she sobbed at length. ' I was in a sore strait, and we were so poor. God had sent more mouths, I thought, than He had sent bread for. Ah, Rex, all the others have been taken from me. Soon there were no mouths at all to be fed, save John's and mine.'

Rex was silent for awhile; then he said with a sigh: 'I am glad I came.'

'And you will stay a little while ?'

'As long as you will, and I can be of help to you.'

'But you will be expected back.'

'No ; they will never expect me.'

'Never ? Have you told ?'

'Yes ! I could not bear the burden. For more than a month I acted a double part and lived a lie; but it became unendurable, and so I told Mr. Brown that I was not his son.'

'And he believed you ?'

'Yes.'

'And did he not ask for proof ?'

'No; he jumped at the truth in a moment. Moreover, he was convinced that if I had not absolute proof of the fact I should not give up all and go out alone in the world.'

She sighed a little and closed her eyes. Then after a few moments, she murmured :

'I am glad he knows. I tried to mend God's work ; but He has pulled all I built to pieces. I have sinned and suffered and schemed for nothing. But perhaps He will make all things right again by-and-by.'

'I did not come here to make myself known,' Rex interposed. 'I will not come between you and my father. If you have kept the secret from him all these years, it is not my place to disclose it.'

Then the tears welled up into her eyes again. 'He knows, Rex,' she said, with trembling lip; 'I felt I could not die easy and not tell him. He did not blame me, Rex. He only said, "Poor Jane! poor Jane!" Oh, he has been a good husband to me—patient amid all my complaining and gentle with all my weaknesses.'

'I am eager to know him,' Rex said. 'Perhaps he will teach me how to paint.'

'You are your father over again,' she said, a proud smile lighting up her pale and wasted face. 'And oh, Rex, he will be so proud of you.'

'I fear not,' he said, with a shake of his head. 'If I could only help him with his pictures I would not mind.'

'Oh ! here he comes,' she said, a bright smile overspreading her face. 'That is John's footstep. I wonder if he will know you or guess who you are ?'

The next moment the door was thrown open and John Raynor entered.

CHAPTER XVIII.

OUT WITH THE TIDE.

'He gave her rest for troublousness ;
And a calm sleep for fitful dreams
Of what is—and of more that seems ;
For tossings upon earth and seas
Gave her to Him where He is.'—*W. M. Rossetti.*

'OH, John, this is Rex !' Jane Raynor said, with a gasp, and she pressed her thin hand to her side as though stabbed with sudden pain.

' Rex ?' he questioned, as though he did not quite understand, and he stood still in the middle of the room.

She tried to speak again; but the words refused to come, while the two men looked at each other in silence.

It was a beautiful face on which the eyes of the younger man rested. Pale and wasted with care and suffering, and furrowed here and there with the march of years, but beautiful still. The full, long beard was plentifully streaked with gray, the hair was thinning above the temples; but none of these things could take from the beauty of the face. Here was the straight, Grecian nose; the thin, refined nostrils; the firm yet gentle mouth; the noble forehead; the large, beautiful eyes, bright with the fire of genius, and liquid with tenderness and kindly feeling.

Rex's heart went out to him in a moment, and he reached out his hand, which John eagerly grasped, and for another moment they stood in silence.

'I have come home to you if you will have me,' Rex struggled to say, while the tears welled up in his eyes and almost blinded him.

John drew his left hand across his own eyes, and trembled visibly.

'God bless you, Rex,' he said; 'I am a proud man to-day.'

Then Jane, who had been silently weeping, broke out into sobs.

'Nay, mother, do not cry,' John said tenderly; 'let us rather rejoice.'

'Yes, yes, John,' she sobbed; 'but let me cry. I am happier now than I have been for twenty years.'

He did not reply, but he went and took her hand in his and stroked it gently, and for awhile only her sobs broke the silence. Then she spoke again.

'Oh, John, it has been a hard struggle; but the day is having a bright ending.'

'We will not talk of the day's ending yet,' he said quietly.

'Yes, yes,' she gasped, 'the day is ending. But Rex has come home. I gave him away because I doubted God. But he will be with you now when I am gone.'

'God has been always with us, Jane.'

'I was thinking of Rex,' she said. 'Come here, my boy, and tell me again you do not hate me.'

'Nay, mother, I cannot hate you,' he said, coming close to her chair. 'Indeed, I love you. You did for the best, I know. Let us forget the past, and start afresh.'

'Nothing can undo the past,' she said; 'the weary years of suffering; the long reproach; the hope deferred. Oh, John! oh, Rex! how I have wronged you both!' and she burst into sobbing again.

'Come, Jane, don't give way so,' John said tenderly; 'we are not upbraiding you.'

'Oh, John, I am not unhappy,' she sobbed; 'indeed, my heart is lighter than ever I expected it would be again. But it does me good to cry.'

She grew composed after awhile, and then the three sat together, and talked in low, hushed voices, about the past and about the future.

'I feel as though at last I had found a home,' Rex said, as the twilight began to deepen around them, and the smouldering fire was stirred in the grate.

'But you were about to make a home of your own, Rex, were you not?' John asked.

'We will say nothing about that now,' Rex said, and then the subject dropped.

But later in the evening, when Jane had been wheeled into an adjoining room by John and a neighbour, who acted as nurse, and laid in her bed, Rex referred to the subject again.

'I did not wish to pain mother,' he said; 'but having to give up Evelyn is nearly the only thing I regret. My young men somebody else will look after; but Evelyn was my all.'

'But need you give her up?' John asked.

'I must give her up now,' he said. 'If I had told her as soon as I knew, I don't think it would have made much difference, for she is not proud; but I deceived her. She will not overlook that. I gave her time to write to me, but she did not write. No, it is all over between us.'

John sighed and was silent.

'My art shall be my bride now,' Rex said after awhile. 'I have always wanted to be a painter; now you will teach me. I have saved most of my salary for the last year or two, and by the time I have spent that I hope to be able to earn something.'

'We will struggle on together somehow,' John answered; 'but painting pictures is a poor business unless one has made a name.'

'Then we must make a name as soon as possible,' Rex answered with a laugh.

John smiled sadly and shook his head. 'Competition is very keen,' he said, 'and a name is not easily made.'

'Well, we will try what we can do, at any rate,' Rex said cheerfully.

'Mother would have saved you from this,' John went on after a pause. 'She meant well by you, Rex, and God only knows how she has suffered. I hadn't the heart to blame her.'

'Perhaps it will all come right in the end,' Rex answered, with a far-away look in his eyes, for his thoughts were back again in Barwich, and he was beginning to pine already for a sight of Evelyn's face.

'She hoped that you, in your riches, would help us, so she told me,' John went on after a pause. 'But she has quite changed in that respect lately. She is so thankful you have come. She would rather have you than money.'

So they talked hour after hour, and as they talked all restraint was broken down, and the heart of each went out to the other. By the time they retired to rest, it almost seemed as though they had known each other always.

Next morning they met each other with a smile and with a warm shake of the hand; and it would be hard to say which was the prouder man of the two. That Rex was proud of his father there could be no doubt, while John was equally proud of his handsome son.

Poor Jane was too ill to leave her bed that day

—the excitement of the previous evening had been too much for her; nor did she ever leave her bed again.

She had caught a severe cold the day she visited Rex at Barwich, for it was very late that night before she reached Aberfae. Inflammation of the lungs soon supervened, and that ended in rapid consumption; and now, as the days passed on, it was clear to all that the tide of her life was ebbing, never to flow again.

None knew this better than she herself. Yet she never murmured. A wonderful change had come over her spirit during the past few weeks. The old hardness and discontent had passed away, and a quiet confidence had taken their place.

Now and then she alluded to the past when Rex was with her. 'Nothing has happened as I planned,' she said one day; 'I have suffered for nothing. You would have been a great painter by this, if you had been with your father always, for John tells me you have wonderful talent.'

'Oh no,' Rex said quickly; 'father takes altogether too bright a view.'

'But it can't be helped now,' she went on, without heeding. 'Some day you will be great in spite of all the hindrances I threw in your way.'

'Oh, please don't worry, mother,' he said kindly; 'I do not blame you at all. Everything, I doubt not, will come out right in the end.'

'You are a good boy, Rex,' she said, her eyes

filling, 'or you would never have forgiven me. I
have nearly wrecked your life as well as my own.
It is a sad come-down for you.'

'Nay, mother; I am really happier here than at
Elmwood. There was no love there, nor welcome,
and if I can brighten your life a bit and father's, I
shall be quite content.'

'Brighten! Oh, Rex, you are the sunshine of
both our lives now. The house is not the same
since you came.'

'If you could only get better, mother!'

'Ah, no,' she sighed, 'that can never be now,
Rex. I have a feeling sometimes that I should
like to be well again. But I know it is best as it
is. You and father will get on better without
me.'

So the days sped on and grew into weeks.
Beautiful May ripened into leafy June, and the
hills all round Aberfae became a picture of loveliness. Rex revelled in the glorious weather and
the beautiful scenery, and wandered hither and
thither making sketches of nooks and glens, which
were a delight to his father.

Meanwhile, John received an offer of fifty pounds
for a picture then on exhibition in a large Lancashire
town. He nearly cried when he got the offer. It
seemed a small fortune to him. 'Rex has turned
the tide for us, mother,' he said to his wife; 'if
you could only get better again, we should have
nothing more to desire.'

'I am very happy, John,' she answered simply.
'We will leave the rest with God.'

Among the villagers, especially the English-
speaking portion of them, speculation was rife as
to who the handsome stranger could be who was
staying with the Raynors. That he was a relative
everyone believed; but what the particular re-
lationship was no one could find out, and neither
John nor Rex felt inclined to gratify their curiosity.

At length it was surmised that he was a nephew
of John's; and as no one was able to contradict
this, or suggest a better explanation, it became
accepted as a fact.

It was near the end of June when Jane Raynor
quietly passed away. The weather had become
intensely hot, and at the last she sank rapidly.
After an exhausting day, she asked to have her
bed drawn up close to the window, that she might
look out over the shining sea once more and watch
the sunset. Away beyond the headland the blue
waters stretched into infinite distance, intersected
by a broad band of light which marked the course
of the setting sun.

It was a beautiful picture, and one that Jane
never tired of. 'It looks like the golden gate of the
better country,' she whispered slowly; 'I think
soon the Lord will let me through.'

Rex had thrown open the window at her request,
that she might feel on her brow the faint, cool
breath of the sea.

'Thank you, my boy,' she said, with a sigh; 'how good you all are to me! But I shall not trouble you very much longer.'

'Nay, do not speak of trouble, mother,' John said tenderly; 'you are no trouble to us.'

For awhile there was silence. Up from the bay came the notes of a quaint, sweet melody. Some fishermen were singing as they were getting ready for a night's fishing.

'They are going out with the tide on the great wide sea,' Jane sighed at length. 'I am going out also. Don't fret, John. Bury me with the children by the yew-tree, on the sunny side of the church-yard. The birds sing there all day long, and I shall sleep content.'

Then silence fell between them again. The sun had disappeared behind the great lone sea, and the twilight was beginning to fall. Rex got up and closed the window, then came and sat by his mother's side.

'You will take care of father, Rex?' she whispered.

'Yes, mother.'

'Now I am content,' she sighed. 'God has forgiven me for the wrong I did, and Christ is with me to lead me home.'

After that she spoke no more. About midnight she opened her eyes and smiled sweetly, then gently fell asleep.

CHAPTER XIX.

A CHANCE MEETING.

'How thrills once more the lengthening chain
  Of memory, at the sight of thee !
Old hopes, which long in dust have lain,
Old dreams, come thronging back again,
  And boyhood lives in me ;
I feel its glow upon my cheek,
  Its fulness of the heart is mine,
As when I leaned to hear thee speak,
  Or raised my doubtful eye to thine.'
Whittier.

THREE years later Rex came face to face with
Evelyn May. He was then settled in London with
his father, and was working hard to master the
mysteries of his art. During all those years Rex
had never seen her, nor even heard of her except
in an indirect way. Often he had longed for a
sight of her sweet, pure face ; but he held himself
in check with a firm hand. He knew his business
was to forget her, if possible—to put the memory of
the past out of his heart, and face the future with
resolute will.

On the day he left Aberfae he was sorely tempted

to go round by Barwich. His heart was hungering for a little news. The months he had been away had seemed like years to him, and he was curious to know what was said in Barwich in explanation of his absence, and whether Evelyn had manifested any grief or concern. He wanted to know also what his young men were doing, and whether the work he had inaugurated was being carried on by anyone else.

But most of all he wanted to see Evelyn once more. If he could look at her beautiful face without himself being seen, he thought it would ease the hunger of his heart. For the inmates of Elmwood he manifested no concern. But Evelyn was his heart's idol, and ever would be ; and to see her face again he fancied would be like receiving a benediction, which he could carry with him into his lonely future.

But he held the desire in check with resolute will. ' I dare not go,' he said. ' I could not see without being seen. I could not hear any news without being recognised.'

It was the beginning of September when they left Aberfae. They began to make preparations for leaving as soon as Jane had been laid to rest in the quiet churchyard.

' I would like to get away from here, Rex,' John said, as they sat together in the lonely house on the night of the funeral. ' Now that you are with me I feel as though I wanted to start afresh. More-

11

over, I want to acknowledge you as my son, which
I cannot do here without exciting a great deal of
talk.   The people here do not know that poor
mother gave up her baby for the sake of gain and
position, and I would like to screen her memory,
for the present at least, from unkind remarks.'

'I am quite willing to go away from here,' Rex
said. 'Indeed, I should prefer it. If one has any
talent, there is not much scope here for its exercise.'

'What do you say to our trying our fortune in
London?' John asked, after a pause.

'I should be delighted,' was the prompt reply.
And so it was settled.   But it took them two months
to get everything ready for their final departure.

Then crept into Rex's heart the passionate longing to go round by way of Barwich. John saw that
something was troubling him, and by-and-by he
got at the truth.

'It is a natural feeling, Rex, my boy,' he said,
with a world of tenderness in his voice. 'But I
think I can help you in some degree.'

'How so?' Rex asked eagerly.

'Well, you can go up to London a little ahead of
me.   You can decide if the rooms Sam Laerton has
selected for us are suitable. If they are, you can
begin unpacking and arranging our tackle. In the
meanwhile I will go round by Barwich and pick up
all the news I can.'

'Splendid!' said Rex; 'I wonder I never thought
of that myself.'

But the news John brought up with him to London gave little comfort to Rex.

'Oh yes, I have heard plenty,' he said, in reply to a question from Rex. 'All sorts of stories are afloat in Barwich. Mr. Brown has been very reticent, it seems, on the subject; but Mrs. Brown and her two daughters have talked very freely, and have frequently contradicted themselves and each other, so that the Barwichians hardly know what to believe. But by most accounts you are a sad scapegrace. It is said that you knew you were not Mr. Brown's son from quite a child, but kept the matter quiet. Mrs. Brown, it seems, ferreted out the secret, and then you had to leave at once. In this matter Mrs. Brown takes great pride for her cleverness, and has been in a chronic state of exultation ever since. But poor Jonas has taken to drinking more heavily than ever, and is fast losing what business shrewdness he once possessed.'

'And my young men?' questioned Rex.

'A number of gentlemen connected with the various churches in the town have formed themselves into a committee, and are carrying on the work with great vigour—at least, so my informant told me.'

'That is satisfactory,' Rex said, after a pause. Then suddenly lifting his eyes, he said, 'And Evelyn? Did you see or hear anything of her?'

'I did not see her,' John said slowly. 'I loitered round by Beechlawn, and even took a ramble up

11—2

through the plantation, but she did not show herself.'

Rex gave a great sigh. All the past came back to him again very vividly. In a moment the present was blotted out, and he was wandering with Evelyn beneath the whispering trees, talking in low tones of a love-lit future. He saw the look of deep content in her beautiful eyes, and felt her fingers tighten on his arm. How her voice thrilled him as she spoke low words of trust and hope, and he bent his head to kiss her lips! Then the dream faded and was gone.

He shook himself at length, and said: 'But you heard of her, father?'

'I heard many things, Rex; but I question if it is worth while to take notice of mere gossip.'

'Yet I should like to know what the gossips say.'

'I don't think you would be any the better for knowing,' John answered.

'Better or not, I must know,' Rex said eagerly.

For a moment or two John was silent.

'Come, you had better tell me what you have heard,' Rex said pleadingly.

'If you *will* hear it, I suppose I must tell you,' John said uneasily; 'but it may be mere gossip. But it is said that both Mrs. May and her daughter are very indignant at the long deception you practised upon them, and that they will not even allow your name to be mentioned in the house. And it is further said that Mrs. May and the Vicar

are anxious for an engagement to bo arranged
between Evelyn and the Vicar's son. Anyhow,
young Leslie is constantly at Beechlawn, and
appears to be favourably received by Miss May.'

' What, so soon ?' groaned Rex; ' surely not.'

' I am only repeating the gossip I heard,' John
said.

' Just so, just so; and yet it may be true—most
likely it is; and, if so, I don't know why it should
matter to me. Why should it ?' and he got up
from his chair and shook himself.

John was silent, nor was the matter referred to
again. Rex was no coward; he knew no good could
come of bemoaning the past. He had had his dream,
now it was over; so let it be. With undaunted
courage he took up his burden and went his way
to meet the future, resolving to be cheerful not only
for his own sake, but for his father's.

To tell the story of their struggles, their hopes,
and fears, and discouragements, during their first
few months in London would be wearisome to the
reader. But neither despaired for a moment.
John found a new inspiration in Rex, and in his
presence worked with a brighter hope. Yielding
to his son's entreaty, he sent his picture, on which
he had been working for months, to the Royal
Academy.

' I know it is useless,' he said; ' but I will do it
to please you.'

' You are too modest and diffident, father,' Rex

said with a laugh. 'I believe it won't be rejected. Anyhow, I know worse pictures will be accepted.'

'Nay, Rex, you think too highly of my pictures,' John said with a smile.

'Nothing venture, nothing have,' Rex replied; 'and you see if I don't turn out a true prophet.'

So the picture was sent, and, much to John's surprise, was accepted. Then a second surprise followed — it wasn't 'skied,' but was well hung, only one remove above the line. This was followed by a third surprise: the picture was singled out by the critics for special praise, and John in a small way found himself quite famous. But the greatest surprise of all was, on private view day, he got a good offer for it and sold it. Had he waited a few days longer till all the critics had had their say, he would have got a much bigger price for it. But he was quite satisfied. He felt that after years of waiting and painstaking labour he had found his feet at last.

John never looked back after that day. He worked with a new confidence, and, as a consequence, revealed a greater power. Assurance took the place of diffidence and timidity. He stood before his easel a master, knowing that at last he knew how to paint.

But Rex refused to be dependent upon his father for support.

'No, father,' he said; 'I must earn my own bread or I shall be miserable.'

So he engaged himself to a large firm of house decorators, and spent three days a week in painting friezes, ceilings, and door-panels; the other three days he spent at his studies, never doubting that with patient endeavour he would win success at last.

When John saw he was determined, he let him have his way. Some people might account such work *infra dig.*, but John Raynor was never troubled with any false pride, and Rex in that respect was his father's own son.

So the months sped on and grew into years, and Rex steadily worked away, earning sufficient as 'house painter,' as Jonas Brown once termed it, to keep him comfortably.

Yet absorbed in his work as he was, Evelyn May never faded out of his memory. He wished sometimes that he could forget her, that he could put aside the past as an unsubstantial dream. But it was not to be. Her face grew into his pictures unconsciously. Her voice haunted his dreams at night.

It is true the old longing to possess her had in some measure passed away. Time had begun to take the sting out of his pain, and he was able to contemplate the past with calmness, if not without regret.

Then all the old longing came back with a rush. He was working on the panels of a drawing-room door in a large house in South Kensington, when the curtains hiding the folding-doors were suddenly pulled aside and two young ladies entered the room.

'You will think it strange our being in the house while it is being decorated,' one said to the other; 'but really this time we could not help ourselves.'

'Oh, well, what does it matter?' was the reply; 'you can live without a drawing-room for a week or two. But are not those panels lovely!'

Rex was too confused to hear the reply, for in the second voice he had recognised the presence of Evelyn May. At the first sound of her voice he had started and turned his head involuntarily, and there, not more than three yards away from him, was the face that to him was the most beautiful on earth.

How he struggled through the ten minutes they remained in the room he never knew. He crept as close to the door as he could, and toyed with his paints and brushes, never daring again to look behind him.

He heard Evelyn praising his work; heard her low laughter that charmed him so much in the years gone by; caught just another glimpse of her sweet pure face as she passed out between the curtains—then silence fell upon the room, and, as it seemed to Rex, darkness also.

CHAPTER XX.

A DAY-DREAM.

'And I have dreamt, in many dreams,
Of her who was a dream to me,
And talked of her by summer streams,
In crowds, and on the sea,
Till in my soul she was enshrined,
A young Egeria of the mind.'

T. K. Hervey.

Rex kept out of his father's way the whole of that evening. He was too agitated to be able successfully to hide it, unless he kept away from watchful eyes. He hardly knew yet how deeply he was stricken; he only felt that he had received a blow which had staggered him, and he wanted to be alone for awhile that he might recover his strength.

He had imagined that he was slowly getting over his love for Evelyn, that time was gradually healing the wound, and that in a year or two at most he would be able to look back upon the past without emotion and without regret. But the experience of this afternoon had shown him how little he knew even of his own heart.

That momentary glimpse of Evelyn's face, the
sweet low music of her voice, had torn away the
thin film from his heart's deep wound, and left him
in hopeless misery and grief. For the first time he
fully realized that his struggle against love was a
hopeless one—that he could not put Evelyn out of
his heart, however much he tried.

He had grown up with her from childhood, had
loved her as a lad, had wooed and won her when
he became a man, and so, by every law of heaven
and earth, she seemed to be his ; and yet he must
not speak to her nor even touch her hand. It
seemed a cruel fate, and yet he would not blame
anyone but himself.

'I lost her through my cowardice,' he moaned, as
he lay tossing on his bed that night. 'If I had told
her as I ought to have done, she would have stood
by me, would have shared my lot with a brave
heart, and helped me in the struggle of life. Oh,
I deserve to be punished.'

And yet it seemed a bitter penalty for one brief
month of deception. Already he had had three
years of suffering, and the struggle, as far as he
could judge, had only just begun.

'Well, well,' he said at length, 'I must fight my
fight and carry my burden. My suffering need not
spoil my life or spoil my work. Nay, the discipline
may make me a better man.'

Yet the discipline did not grow less trying as the
days passed on. Whenever he got away from his

work, her face haunted him, and even when he stood before his easel with palette and brush in hand, he would sometimes fall to dreaming, and the canvas before him would melt and vanish, and there would come up before him a vision of sunny fields, and a low hill crowned with trees, and a woodland path with the sunlight flickering on the mossy floor, and a fair maiden coming to meet him as he stood leaning against the stile.

How strangely events shape themselves! That dream, so often repeated, was the beginning of Rex's fame. He commenced the picture to please himself. He thought if he placed his dream on canvas it might cease to haunt him. So it grew slowly from week to week and month to month. It was no 'pot-boiler,' he never intended it for the public gaze. He painted it to ease his heart, and so he put his life into it, his very soul.

No fear of public criticism ever held his hand in check. No thought of the 'schools' affected his method. He painted for himself; the technique was his own. Perhaps for these very reasons the picture was so great a success. At first he would not hear of sending it to the Academy. He saw no particular merit in it, he said. It was only a study. He had painted it as a pastime more than anything else. 'It is full of faults; the critics will jump upon it. Besides'—and this seemed an all-sufficient reason —'the public will never understand it.'

But Rex's friends over-ruled all his objections.

His father was particularly anxious that it should be sent.

'I tell you, Rex,' he said, 'it will be one of the pictures of the year.' And so it proved. Rex awoke one morning and found himself famous. 'At the Stile' was the talk of the town. It was not only the artistic merit of the picture that so commended it; it appealed to the heart as well as the head. The touch of nature in it was so true and so real that people lingered over it with half-pathetic gaze. In many a heart it recalled a memory of the past. It seemed a bit of real life put on canvas. It was clear to all that the heart of the painter was in his work.

Rex received the congratulations of his friends with great composure. He did not seem at all elated by his success. For his father's sake he was glad; for himself he had little care. If only Evelyn were his, how different the world would be! for her sake he would have rejoiced in growing power and fame. But since she was lost to him, what did it matter?

Nor was that all he had to depress him just then. For several weeks past the papers had been full of the failure of the great Imperial National and Cosmopolitan Bank. Jonas Brown was a ruined man, and not only ruined financially—he was also disgraced. The revelations of reckless speculations which appeared in the newspapers day by day were painful reading to Rex, and, indeed, to

"'I tell you, Rex,' he said, 'it will be one of the pictures of the year.'"

thousands of others, for the collapse of the Imperial National and Cosmopolitan meant ruin and destitution to hundreds of families.

Close upon the crash followed accounts of the arrest of Jonas Brown and his fellow-directors. Then came particulars of the trial, which we need not here recapitulate, for they will be fresh in the memory of many of our readers.

Poor Jonas, on account of his age and the broken state of his health, was sentenced to only six months' imprisonment. But no one who saw him in the dock that day believed he would come out of the prison alive.

Rex could hardly help shedding tears as he read of his old friend's sad fate. In his heart there was a warm place for Jonas still. The old man, in spite of ill-temper and coarse abuse, had been kind to him in many ways, and would have been kinder, perhaps, but for his wife.

He could not forget his last interview with him, and how sorry Jonas seemed to give him up; had even hinted at adopting him, and perhaps would have attempted to do so but for Mrs. Brown. All this was not lost upon Rex. He forgot the loneliness and neglect of all those years at Elmwood, and remembered only the kindnesses he had received.

'I would like to help him if I could,' Rex said to his father one day when talking the matter over. 'He has a claim upon me.'

'And upon me also,' John answered with a

far-away look in his eyes. 'In the old days, Rex, before we left Barwich, he was very good to us, and at a time when we sorely needed help.'

'Yes, yes,' Rex said absently; 'but we can do nothing now. We must wait till he comes out of prison.'

So it was resolved that Rex should meet him when his term of imprisonment was ended, and help him in the way that would seem best at the time.

In the meanwhile both father and son went steadily on with their work. John's health had considerably improved since the burden of poverty had been lifted from his shoulders. Moreover, his work had become a greater pleasure to him now that he felt master of his craft and was sure of a sale for his pictures.

If only Jane were alive to share his prosperity, he felt he would desire nothing more on earth. And sometimes he sighed to himself a little bit sadly, that she had been taken away just as the sky was beginning to brighten and Rex had come home to cheer their lives.

'Poor mother!' he would sometimes say to himself; 'life was very hard for her. She did for the best, as she thought, and kept hoping for better days, and when the better days came she died.'

Rex sometimes thought that his father's heart was back in the little graveyard at Aberfae, where slept his wife and the children. It was not often he spoke of the children; they had died young, but they had left a gap in his heart which would never be filled on earth.

On the whole, however, the winter wore pleasantly away. They lived in a good house now, and had a kind old housekeeper to look after them, besides which they had made troops of friends. Rex Raynor was the coming man in the art world, and, as a consequence, friends crowded round him on every side.

*   *   *   *   *

It was a bitterly cold day in February when Rex found himself once more in Liverpool. He could hardly realize that he had been away from it nearly five years. He might not have been away five weeks, for nothing had changed, or next to nothing. The same names were over the shops, the same goods in the windows for any difference he could see; the same buses were in the streets — ay, and the very same drivers, looking scarcely any older.

He almost fancied that he was still a clerk in the bank, and that he had dreamed all the rest. The only strange thing was, nobody recognised him. Walking down Lord Street and up Church Street he saw a dozen familiar faces. Once or twice he was on the point of speaking, but suddenly remembered himself and passed on. It was evident that five years had changed him; his thick brown beard seemed a complete disguise.

It was too cold, however, to loiter in the streets,

so he hurried off to his hotel to make arrangements for the morrow. On the following morning at eight o'clock, Jonas Brown was to be liberated from Kirkdale Gaol, and he was anxious that there should be no mishap.

Friday morning, the fourth of February, could scarcely be said to 'break' at all. The fog-laden atmosphere struggled with the daylight and kept it at bay. The wind blew keen and bitter from the east, bringing with it occasional dashes of sleet, which unmistakably betokened snow. Clustered about the gloomy portal of Kirkdale Gaol, a small knot of people had gathered, chiefly of the lowest order, who had come to give a welcome to their pals or their relatives on their release, and to celebrate the occasion by getting drunk at one of the public-houses across the way.

Punctually at eight o'clock the heavy door was thrown open, and about twenty people filed through: some with a laugh and a skip, some slowly, muttering sullen oaths; others with a jaunty air, as though they were superior to the common herd.

In a few moments they had disappeared—most of them within the doors of the brilliantly-lighted public-houses with which the neighbourhood abounds. Only one was left alone in the street—an old man, and, apparently, forsaken. He was the last to appear, for he walked with a feeble step, and when the door closed behind him he stood still and shivered in the bitter east wind.

The others had friends to meet them, or had some place to go to. He had neither. He was alone and homeless. It seemed almost a cruel thing to turn him out of his warm cell and push him into the wintry street. The cold appeared to chill his very blood, and he looked helplessly first in one direction, then in another.

A few yards away was a cab with a policeman standing by the door. He was evidently interested in the old man, for he watched him narrowly. At length he went up to him and spoke.

'You are Mr. Jonas Brown, I think.'

'Yes,' said Jonas, looking at him in surprise; 'do you want me?'

'Well, an old acquaintance of yours would like you to come and have breakfast with him at his hotel, and talk matters over.'

'An old acquaintance?' said Jonas, in astonishment. 'Who is he—where is he?'

'He is at the North-Western Hotel, but who he is I don't know. Will you go?'

'Go?' and Jonas shivered; 'yes, man, I'll go anywhere. I'm alone. God help me!'

Rex was anxiously waiting Jonas's arrival. But when the door was thrown open and the old man tottered in, he drew back with a gasp of surprise. What a change five years had wrought! He looked twenty years older, and so feeble that he seemed ready to fall.

Rex took his hand in silence and led him to an

easy-chair by the fire, then settled with the policeman, and closed and locked the door.

Jonas watched him with a curious look in his
eyes, and when Rex came and took a chair on the
opposite side of the fire, he said :

'I don't understand this no road. I don't know
who you are, and what you can want with me I
can't understand.'

'I wish to befriend you, if possible,' Rex said,
trying to disguise his voice. 'I thought you might
not have many friends. People who are down are
not overburdened with friends as a rule.'

'Friends ! God help me !' and Jonas shook his
head sadly. 'I didn't know I had a friend left ;'
and the old man's lip quivered visibly.

'I thought that might be the case,' Rex said after
a pause, for Jonas's emotion had touched him
deeply ; 'and so I came over to see if I might be
of any service to you.'

'But I don't know you,' Jonas said, brushing his
hand across his eyes, 'and yet your voice sounds
familiar, too.'

'You knew me once,' said Rex, 'and you have
been kind to me and mine, and I would like to
repay your kindness in some way, if that is
possible.'

'Kind to you ? Nay, nay, I've never been very
much given to kindness. I've sowed seed of a
different sort all through my life. Ay, an' I've
reaped the harvest too.'

'But you were kind to me,' said Rex, 'and it's only fair you should reap the harvest of that as well.'

But Jonas did not reply; he only looked at him with increasing wonder in his eyes.

'And you don't recognise me yet?' Rex questioned.

'No,' said Jonas, with a shake of the head; 'I can't make you up. I have no glasses, you see, an' my sight is getting very poor.'

Rex drew his chair closer to him.

'In the old days you called me Rex,' he said; 'now you know me.'

'Rex!' Jonas said, struggling to his feet. 'You, Rex? God help me, so you are!' and he fell upon his neck and burst into tears.

'Oh, Rex, Rex,' he said, struggling with his emotion; 'I don't deserve this, I really don't. I—I——'

'No, don't blame yourself,' Rex said. 'We will let the past go for the present, and while we are having some breakfast we will talk of the future.'

CHAPTER XXI.

LIFE'S LITTLE DAY.

'But now the night is round my feet,
   Now stars are looking in my eyes;
   Now from the vale and stream there rise
Remoter influences, replete
With heart-pang lulled to bitter-sweet.'
                                   W. M. Rossetti.

JONAS sat down before the toothsome meal Rex had provided; but he could not eat.

'It ain't no good, Rex,' he said; 'I ain't in the eatin' line to-day. I'm never hungry now as I used to be, and, besides, I've a lump in my throat which I can't swallow. It's all so unexpected like. I lay awake all last night wonderin' what would become of me. I thought perhaps I might get into the workhouse or into the river. I never thought of this.'

Rex did not reply, and Jonas rambled on:

'Not that I wanted to drown myself, for that seems a cowardly way of gettin' out of the world. But neither, for that matter, do I care about living.

The game ain't worth the candle, Rex. Life's a fraud. It's nothing but struggle and wriggle, and push and checkmate, from beginnin' to end. I've had my day. At first I was too cute for most of 'em, an' generally got the upper hand; but latterly folks 'ave been too cute for me. I oughtn't to grumble, I suppose. I've only been paid back in my own coin. Folks generally gets their rights in the long-run, Rex.'

'Yes, I believe they do,' Rex said thoughtfully.

'Ay, it's a queer world,' Jonas went on. 'Your mother used to say—nay, not your mother, Rex; but you know who I mean—she used to say that doin' right always prospered in the end. Maybe she was right. I've thought a good deal about what she used to say to me, durin' the last six months. It's funny how the past comes back sometimes. Well, well. It's the only bit in my life that is worth remembering. It was a sad day for me when she was taken. Nothing has ever gone right since.'

'She was a beautiful woman,' Rex said, more to himself than to Jonas.

'Ay, she were too good for me; I always know'd that. An' the contrast between her an' the other one—well, I oughtn't to say anything, I suppose. You knew 'em both, Rex.'

'Do you know where Mrs. Brown is?' Rex questioned after a pause.

'Nay, I don't know, an' I don't care. She's safe

enough you may depend. She must have saved thousands of pounds out of her housekeeping money. I never know'd her equal.'

Then for awhile silence fell between them. Rex's thoughts were back in Barwich again, and his heart was aching for news of Evelyn. A year and a half had elapsed since he caught that momentary glimpse of her face, and since then he had heard no word of her. Was she married, he wondered, or was she still single? Did she still live at Barwich, or had she and her mother gone south, as they sometimes talked of doing? Jonas had lived at Elmwood up to nine months ago: he would probably know.

'I suppose everything has gone on much as usual at Barwich since I left?' Rex said at length.

'Ay, things haven't changed much,' Jonas said gloomily.

'Is Mrs. May still at Beechlawn? And Evelyn; is she still unmarried?'

'I expect the gal is married by this. There's been talk about it long enough,' Jonas grunted.

'It is a fact, then, that she is engaged to Stuart Leslie?' Rex questioned.

'I suppose so; I don't know. They don't live much at Barwich now. A few months in the summer, and then they're off again. It's a good job Mrs. May did not entrust her money with me as she thought of doing once. I wish I had stuck to the cotton; I should have saved myself and a lot of other people a deal of trouble;' and Jonas brushed his hand quickly across his eyes.

'Well, it's no use crying over spilt milk,' Rex said at length. 'To-morrow you shall go home with me if you will. While I live and have my health you shall be cared for. So don't fret about the past any more than you can help.'

For awhile Jonas was silent. He was evidently trying to swallow the lump in his throat, and was not succeeding very well in the attempt. Every now and then he tried to speak, but the words would not come. At length he got up from his seat, and staggered to his easy-chair by the fire, into which he dropped with a sudden jerk. Then he seized the poker and made a dive at a lump of coal; after which he seemed to recover himself.

'I can't say nothin', Rex,' he said, with his old defiance of grammar; 'I'll do anything you tell me.'

So the next day saw Jonas comfortably settled in his new home. John received him with great kindness, not to say courtesy, and did his best to make him feel at home. Jonas was evidently deeply touched by the kindness he received; but he said little. He was too feeble and broken down to talk much; nor did he seem to recover his strength as the days passed on.

For a whole month he never left his room. He was content to sit in his easy-chair, staring into the fire. Of the pictures he saw in the glowing grate he did not speak. Sometimes a tear would start in his eye and roll silently down his withered cheek; sometimes he would smile a wintry smile, but not often. For the most part he sat in moody silence, with a far-away look in his eyes, as though his thoughts were back in the past, and as though the present had for him no interest and no concern.

As the spring advanced he recovered his strength a little, and on sunshiny days would steal quietly up into the large studio and watch John and Rex at their work. But it was very evident that he would never again be the man he had been. Not only was his health broken, but his spirit was broken as well; he had lost completely his old domineering manner. In many things he was just like a child.

John and Rex did their best to cheer him, but with poor success. At first they tried to get him interested in pictures, but soon gave up the attempt. Jonas cared no more for pictures than in the old days, while in his heart he had a secret contempt for those who painted them. According to his judgment, it was a sad waste of time, and a miserable way of trying to earn a living.

'An' you really make money out of a job like that?' he said to Rex one day when they were alone in the studio.

'Yes, we make enough to keep us very comfortably,' Rex answered with a smile.

'Humph, I should think you'd rather be an 'ouse-painter.'

'Well, I was a house-painter for a year or two,' Rex laughed; 'but I gave it up when I found I could paint pictures.'

'You did, eh? I don't think I should;' and Jonas again relapsed into silence.

When the Raynors had company, he persistently kept out of sight.

'I don't want to see nobody,' he would say, 'an' I don't want nobody to see me. Of course, Rex, if you very much wish me to come down, I will. But I'd rather not; I'm happier alone. I sit an' look into the fire an' dream. Sometimes it seems as if something or somebody comes an' talks to me; I can't understand it. But an easier feeling comes into my heart, and I think there may be another life than this, where a fellow will have another chance. May used to think so. Perhaps it's she as comes an' talks to me; I don't know. Only I'd rather be quiet, Rex, if you don't mind.'

So Jonas would be left to his thoughts, and to the workings of that good spirit that never forsakes any of earth's poor children.

Meanwhile the Royal Academy was once more thrown open, and Rex's picture had again a place of honour. The critics said it marked a distinct advance on his picture of the previous year, and furnished undeniable evidence of the young artist's **genius and skill.** Great things were predicted of

him should his life be spared. Indeed, one or two
papers prophesied that he was destined to become
the most notable painter of the century. On the
other hand, however, a few well - known critics
declared that they saw no merit in his pictures at
all, and insinuated that though he had gone up
like a rocket, he would come down like a stick.

But Rex went quietly on his way, unmoved by
either praise or blame. He sometimes wondered
whether Evelyn ever read the papers, and if she
did, what she thought of the honours that had
been crowded upon him. A smile from her at that
time, or a kind word, would have been more to him
than all the praise of his brother artists, and all the
laudations of the press. In his heart she still
reigned supreme.

Naturally he was much sought after, and now
and then he went into company. But of all the
faces he saw, none to his fancy could compare with
hers. Through years of silence and misunderstand-
ing his love lived on. He might be forgotten, but
he could not forget. Evelyn had ceased to love
him, so he believed. But his love had grown rather
than diminished. She was still his heart's desire.

In this respect he was a surprise to himself. He
was constantly on the look-out for her, even against
his will. On private view day he scanned far more
eagerly the faces of the crowd than he did the
pictures on the walls, and when on rare occasions
he went into company, he always wondered if she

would be present, and invariably returned to his home with the old hunger gnawing at his heart.

So another summer wore slowly away, and autumn at length began to steal silently over the land, and with the browning leaf Jonas began to droop and die. He had never gathered any real strength, never recovered his spirits; and now in the shortening days he took to his bed, owning that he was 'beaten,' though never uttering a word of complaint.

He felt that his life was drawing to its close, and neither John nor Rex attempted to buoy him up with any false hopes of recovery. He was very patient, and wonderfully gentle for one who was naturally peevish and irritable. His troubles had subdued him to a degree one could scarcely have imagined.

Rex declined all invitations, and spent his evenings at home with Jonas. The old man liked to have Rex with him.

'You are very good, Rex,' he would sometimes say. 'I don't deserve it, I really don't. But you make me very happy, all the same.'

'I want to make you happy,' Rex would say. 'I don't want you to have a trouble or a care.'

And the tears would roll down Jonas's withered cheeks, and in silence he would press Rex's hand for answer.

As the end drew near, Rex wanted to send for a minister. But Jonas would not hear of it.

'I'd rather talk with you, Rex,' he said. 'You know me best, an' since you've been so good to me, perhaps God won't turn me away.'

'I'm sure He won't,' Rex answered.

'And you can pray with me now and then. I like to hear you pray, Rex. You've been a good lad, an' you'll get paid for it in the long-run.'

'You've only seen the best side of me,' Rex answered.

'Nay, lad, I've seen pretty well into thy heart. But never mind that. I'm going away now. My life's been a great mistake, Rex. If I could live it over again, I think I would do differently. The little good I ever did has come back in blessings a thousand-fold. If I had sown more corn and fewer tares, Rex, the reapin' ud be different. We reap as we sow, boy; I've found that out.'

For a day or two before the end he scarcely spoke a word. Rex and John kept patient watch by his bedside, and now and then Jonas tried to smile his gratitude.

He passed away in the night. Rex was sitting by his side.

'Are you there, Rex?' the words came in a feeble whisper.

'Yes, I am here,' Rex answered, bending over him. 'Can I do anything for you?'

'Speak to me those words again,' he whispered. 'You know, Rex.'

And Rex spoke slowly the words the old man

had learned to love: 'For God so loved the world that He gave His only begotten Son, that whosoever believeth in Him should not perish, but have everlasting life.'

He did not speak again. For a moment a feeble smile flickered over his face, like a gleam of winter sunshine, then suddenly vanished, and with the vanishing smile the spirit went out in the night to the God who gave it birth.

CHAPTER XXII.

STRANGERS YET.

'Oh, pleasant days of hope—for ever flown !
    Could I recall you !—but that thought is vain.
Availeth not persuasion's sweetest tone
    To lure the fleet-winged travellers back again ;
Yet fair, though faint, their images shall gleam,
Like a bright rainbow on an evening stream.'
                                        S. T. Coleridge.

IN one of his conversations with Rex, Jonas had expressed a desire to be buried at Barwich by the side of his dead wife, and now that he was dead, both father and son were anxious to carry out his request. It would entail trouble and considerable expense, but they did not mind that.

'I should like to be buried with Jane and the children down at Aberfae when I die,' John said. 'And it is only right that Jonas should sleep by the wife he loved.'

So a letter was sent off at once to Mr. Leslie, the Vicar of Barwich, and by return of post an answer was received saying that everything possible should be dono at Barwich for the purpose of carrying out the late banker's wish.

'Let me also,' the letter went on, 'express a deep sense of the relief I feel, that poor Mr. Brown found such an asylum during the closing days of his life. I have often wondered, along with many others, what had become of him. I knew that he had served his term of imprisonment and left the gaol alive. But after that no trace of him could be found. I will not say that any of us made very diligent search for him. Perhaps we were all too ready to forget him. Some of my parishioners had lost their all through him, and naturally enough resented even the mention of his name. But to me it is a matter of intense relief to find that in his disgrace and feebleness he was cared for, and that now he is to be buried alongside his wife, whom, no doubt, he fondly loved. Furthermore, let me say, how all the Barwichians rejoice in the growing fame of your son' (the letter was to John). 'In the hearts of the people he has always lived. His going away, on the discovery of his identity, was a real grief to everyone; though to go away was, no doubt, under the circumstances, a proper thing to do. But we shall feel honoured by his presence amongst us on Wednesday next, though the occasion of his coming is such a sad one. I await your further orders, which shall have prompt attention.'

Rex read the letter with a frown upon his handsome face, and felt half disposed not to go to

Barwich at all. It would be a painful ordeal in
many respects to stand there in the churchyard to
be stared at. On the other hand, it would be a
real joy to look again upon the scenes so dear to
his memory and around which clustered so many
happy associations. But whether the pleasure or
the pain would be greater he was unable to
determine.

There was one consideration, however, which
determined him. He might see Evelyn. That in
itself was a prospect he could not resist. Two years
had passed away since he caught that momentary
glimpse of her face, and his heart felt starved for
another sight of her. He knew it was foolish to
give way to such a feeling, but he could not help
it. Day after day and week after week he had
kept hoping that by some strange chance he might
see her. He knew that she came frequently to
London. At least, she used to do, and it was no
unreasonable thing to suppose he might now and
then stumble across her path. He was frequently
meeting people he knew from Barwich and Liverpool in Fleet Street, Piccadilly, and the Strand,
though none of them ever recognised him, and he
never made himself known. But with that one
exception, Evelyn, he had never met. In every
place of public resort which he visited, he looked
eagerly for the one face that was fairer and dearer
to him than any other face on earth. But it seemed
as though the fates were unkind to him. Other

well-known faces he occasionally saw, but hers never.

He did not question himself as to what possible good could come of his meeting her. He knew if he saw her at Barwich the chances were she would not recognise him. But even though she looked scorn and contempt at him, he had a feeling that the sight of her face would appease in some degree his heart's hunger, and that he would go on his way better satisfied. Had he attempted to reason the matter out, he would probably have come to the very opposite conclusion.

It was a sweet, restful day in late September when the funeral took place—one of those strangely quiet days when it would almost seem as though tired Nature had dropped asleep. The brown leaves hung motionless upon the trees. The wind had died away into utter stillness. Even the insects had ceased to hum.

In the old churchyard, surrounded by tall and stately elms, the silence could be felt. The town of Barwich was not near enough for its voice to be heard. For some unaccountable reason it had grown away from the church, and so the quiet graveyard remained quite as much in the country as when Barwich was only a village.

The voice of Mr. Leslie sounded strangely solemn as he commenced the service at the grave: 'Man that is born of a woman hath but a short time to live, and is full of misery.'

13

Rex took off his hat and cast a swift glance
around him. A crowd of people had assembled—
far more than had been in the church. But as yet
he had seen no individual face. He had come with
his father from the station in a closed carriage.
He had walked into the church without looking
to the right or to the left; had seen no one while
the service had proceeded within the building;
but now, in that swift glance around him, one face,
fair and beautiful, stood out clear and distinct from
all the rest—the face of Evelyn.

His heart gave a great throb, and then for a
moment seemed to stop. He felt himself grow pale
even to the lips. But he did not dare to raise his
eyes again during the service. In dreamy mono-
tone the Vicar's voice sounded in his ears. But he
scarcely heard any of the words he said. He felt
all the while that over against him Evelyn May
was standing, her eyes fixed upon his face.

Why had she come ? he wondered. He knew it
was not often that people in her walk in life put in
an appearance at a funeral. Had she come out of
curiosity ?—out of respect for the memory of Jonas
Brown ?—to have a look at her old lover ?—to
mark the changes time had wrought in him ?—or
to show him how different she was, and how completely she had outlived the past ?

The service ended at length. The Vicar stole
away through the crowd back to his vestry. There
was a general movement and shuffle of feet. Rex

replaced his hat and looked round him once more. Evelyn was standing in the same place, very pale, but beautiful as ever. On her left stood her mother, looking a little older, but a lovely woman still. And close to her right hand was Stuart Leslie, with a smile, partly triumphant, partly malicious, upon his handsome face.

The smile was not lost upon Rex, but his eyes instantly wandered back again to Evelyn's face. It was the face that for years he had longed to see, and they might not meet again for years. They might not meet again for ever.

She met his gaze without flinching, but without the least sign of recognition. But in her great solemn eyes there was a look he could not understand. Was it pity? Was it reproach? Was it scorn? Perhaps it was the latter. Yet there was no scorn upon her face. Her lips were sweet and gentle as of old.

She had scarcely altered at all in the five years he had been away. She was a little more stately, perhaps. Her figure was a little fuller and rounder; her face a shade more grave. In other respects she was the Evelyn of old—the beautiful maiden who had won his love, and who had promised to be his wife.

Did she wait, he wondered, for him to show some sign of recognition? No, that could not be. He had been the offender. He had deceived her when he ought to have been true. And so she would never forgive him. He felt the hot blood rush to his face as the memory of the past swept over him, and, dropping his eyes, he whispered something to his father, then turned quickly on his heel and followed the Vicar.

Mr. Leslie was very gracious with him. Would he and his father stay and dine with him and spend the night at the Vicarage ? He would like to have a little talk with him about pictures, especially Rex's latest success. He was proud that a Barwichian had won so much fame. And then it was very noble of him and his father to befriend poor Mr. Brown in the way they had done. He would be delighted to have a very long talk about things in general, so much had happened in the last five years. Could he not spend a night in Barwich and visit some of his old friends ?

But Rex was firm. ' We have arranged to return by the next train,' he said ; ' I have only just time to pay the fees, then perhaps you would not mind letting me out by the side-door, and I will take the footpath to the station and so avoid the crowd.'

' But your father ?' the Vicar questioned.

' He has gone round the other way in the carriage.'

At the churchyard gate, near the Vicarage, Mrs. May and Evelyn waited—waited till the crowd had all dispersed, then turned slowly round and retraced their steps up the churchyard path.

Did they wait in the hope of seeing Rex ? If so,

they were disappointed. They saw the Vicar come out of the church alone, and take the short cut, by a narrow footpath, to his house. Then they, too, left the churchyard, stepped into their carriage, which was waiting at the gate, and drove home.

Meanwhile Rex and his father were speeding back to London. But very little was said during the weary journey. John, indeed, slept most of the way, for they were the only occupants of a first-class compartment, and John was very tired.

Rex was not at all sorry to be left in silence. He was in no mood for conversation, the events of the day had been too depressing. In one thing he had realized his desire; he had seen Evelyn, but he was no happier for it. Nay, if possible, his heart ached more stubbornly than ever.

He had never admitted, even to himself, that he had cherished the faintest hope that he would win again Evelyn May. At the first he told his father that Evelyn was utterly lost to him. He believed it then; he had believed it ever since. Yet, notwithstanding this, he was sorely disappointed with their meeting to-day. She might have given him, he thought, some faint glance of recognition, some token of forgiveness. It was hard to feel the reproach of her eyes, and to carry the memory of it as long as he lived.

If any lingering hope had remained in his heart, it was rooted out now. He felt, as he had never felt before, how great was the gulf between them.

After five years and more they had met as strangers, without even a glance of recognition; as strangers they had parted. So another page in his life's history was ended, so the last link that bound him to the old life was snapped for evermore.

CHAPTER XXIII.

GROUND FOR HOPE.

'The ancient sorrow now is not,
　　Since time can heal the keenest smart;
Yet the vague memory, scarce forgot,
　　Lingers deep down within the heart.'
　　　　　　　　　　　　　Lewis Morris.

EVELYN and her mother drove home in silence.
On reaching Beechlawn, Evelyn went at once to
her own room and locked the door. She wanted
to be alone, to read her own heart again as she had
tried to do many times before.

Drawing an easy-chair close up to the window,
which was open, she sat down and rested her elbow
on the sill, while her eyes went wandering away
across the billowy landscape which spread far away
before her. It was a familiar scene, and one of
which she never tired. Yet to-day she paid little
heed to its beauty. Her thoughts were in other
directions, her heart aching with a load that seemed
to grow heavier all the while.

It had cost her an effort to go to the churchyard

and stand face to face with the man to whom she
had given her heart, and who, to all appearances,
had forgotten her, and who wished himself to be
forgotten. It was a very perplexing problem. She
wanted to think of him with all charity, for he had
been her youthful ideal, and even now, in spite of
his long silence and seeming neglect, he held the
first place in her heart. He was her first love, and
she had a feeling that she could never love another
as she had loved him.

Her mother had tried to dissuade her from going
to the funeral. She had taken all along a less
charitable view of the matter than Evelyn had.
Fond as she had been of Rex, she could not quite
forgive what seemed his studied silence and all too
palpable inconsistency. She knew that Evelyn
had written to him on receipt of his letter, and as
the letter had never been returned, very naturally
supposed it had reached its proper destination;
and seeing that he had never responded to it—
that he had gone away without letting anyone
know of his whereabouts—that he had permitted
the months and years to pass away without seeking
any reconciliation—the very natural inference was,
that he wished to be forgotten as he wished to
forget.

How much Evelyn suffered no one ever knew,
for she resolutely locked up her trouble in her
heart and went about her daily duties as though
nothing had happened. But though outwardly

calm and unmoved, the inward pain and heart-break could not be altogether hidden from her mother's watchful eyes. As the summer advanced, she grew pale and listless. Every day she kept hoping that Rex would come back to her, and every evening added a fresh disappointment to the many that had preceded it.

One day her mother found her seated by the open window, with hollow, hungry-looking eyes, and tears upon her cheeks, and at sight of her suffering she could restrain her indignation no longer.

'You are thinking of Rex,' she said, with so much bitterness in her tone that Evelyn looked up in surprise.

'Yes, mother, I am,' she said quietly. 'Is it any matter of surprise that I should ?'

'No, not a matter of surprise; but it would be well if you could forget him. I wish you would try. This trouble is killing you.'

'It is not easy to forget, mother,' was the quiet answer.

'I don't know. A man who has treated you as he has done is not worth remembering.'

'Hush, mother!' she said, rising to her feet and clasping her hands. 'We may not know all; perhaps some day the mystery will be cleared up.'

'But you cannot deny, Evelyn, that he was party to an imposture for some considerable time.'

'He admits that himself. It is that which troubles him, and has driven him away. He thinks I will not forgive him.'

'How can he think that after the letter you sent to him? Or, if he had any doubts, why did he not wait and see you? No, Evelyn, young men are proverbially fickle, and Rex is no exception to the rule.'

'And you think he has grown tired of our engagement, and is anxious to be rid of me?'

'What else can I think?' Mrs. May answered, with a flash of indignation in her gentle eyes. 'Put him out of your thoughts, Evelyn, as one unworthy. Forget him as quickly as you can.'

'No, mother, not yet,' she answered, with quiet dignity. 'I know he is not perfect, but he is not what you would have me believe him.'

'Ah, well,' Mrs. May answered with a sigh; 'I would not think unjustly of him, but facts are eloquent as well as stubborn.'

'We may not have all the facts,' Evelyn said quietly, and then sank into her chair again.

For a moment or two her mother looked at her with yearning, anxious eyes, then turned and left the room.

But as the months and years passed away, she returned to the charge again and again. It seemed clear enough to her that Rex had deliberately thrown over her child, and he the son of a nameless painter—the child of a woman who had de-

scended to fraud and deception of the worst kind.
To her it was humiliating in the extreme. She
wondered that Evelyn's pride did not come to her
rescue. If he were someone of noble birth, it
would be less galling. But to be thrown over and
made the sport of one who was without name
or position made her blood tingle to her finger-
tips.

But Evelyn was generally silent during her
mother's indignant outbursts.

Once she replied, with quiet dignity: 'He was
no adventurer, mother, as you know. He grew up
with us from childhood; as a boy he was the soul
of honour, and when he became a man he was ever
chivalrous and true, and it cannot be that he
changed his nature in a moment.'

'You are stubborn, Evelyn, and in this matter
unreasonable,' her mother answered. 'But sup-
posing he is all you have pictured him, he evidently
wishes the engagement to end, and seeing there
are others good as he is in every way, who would
cultivate your acquaintance, I think——'

'Please say no more, mother,' Evelyn answered
quickly. 'You hurt me by such allusions.'

But Mrs. May, having set her heart upon an
object, was not easily discouraged. She had seen
all along that Stuart Leslie was fond of Evelyn,
and though he was neither so manly nor so handsome as Rex, yet he was handsome enough, and
rich enough, and clever enough to please most

people, and, indeed, from a worldly point of view,
might be considered a very good match.

Moreover, since Rex was out of the way, Mrs.
May had promised Stuart she would do all she
could to further his suit. She had a feeling that
she would be much more content if she could see
her daughter comfortably settled. As matters
stood, if anything happened to her, Evelyn would
be alone in the world, and such a prospect troubled
her sometimes. Evelyn was her only care, and her
happiness her one concern.

But though Evelyn was friendly enough with
Stuart, and liked him in a general way, the idea of
his playing the part of lover was most distasteful
to her.

Notwithstanding this, however, he went more
frequently than ever to the house, and when the
rumour got abroad in Barwich that he and Evelyn
were engaged, he never attempted to deny it. So
it grew into a settled conviction in the minds of
the Barwichians, that sooner or later Evelyn and
young Leslie would be married.

When Evelyn first heard the report she was very
indignant, and insisted on going away from home
at once, and, indeed, from that day forward she
spent less and less time at Beechlawn.

During one of Stuart Leslie's visits, and just on
the eve of Evelyn and her mother's departure for
the Riviera, Mrs. May said to him: ' You must be
patient, Stuart. Evelyn will not be coerced.'

'But she gives me no encouragement at all,' he said petulantly.

'She must forget Rex before she will encourage you,' was the answer. 'And I am helping her all I can to forget him.'

'But 'pon my soul, excuse me, but it's terribly hard on a fellow.'

'Perhaps it is,' Mrs. May answered with a smile. 'Still, the discipline may be good for you.'

'Discipline be——' Then he checked himself suddenly.

'Stuart, you must not lose control of yourself,' Mrs. May said severely.

'And you must not be hard upon a fellow,' was the quick rejoinder.

'I am not hard,' was the reply. 'On the contrary, I have encouraged you all I could.'

'Will you be away long?' he asked after a pause.

'Three months at least, perhaps four.'

'The dev—that is—really, Mrs. May, you will not stay away so long. What am I to do?'

'Learn self-control, Stuart, and get through your examinations.'

He bit his lip in silence, and soon after took his departure.

At length came news of Rex's sudden leap into fame, and hope revived in Evelyn's heart once more, for she thought: 'He has been poor and nameless all these years, and perhaps felt in his changed circumstances that he had no right to aspire to me; but now that he has won for himself a position and can meet me on equal terms, perhaps he will come back. Oh! I hope he will.'

But though she watched and waited, he did not come, and slowly but surely the conviction began to eat its way into her heart:

'He does not want me. Mother has been all along right in her surmise.'

But she kept her fears to herself, and nursed her grief in silence. Moreover, time, the great healer, had in some measure taken the sting out of her disappointment, and all unconsciously dimmed the memory of those bygone years.

She had never seen Rex but once since he went away, and then she did not know it was him. She only caught a momentary glimpse of the young painter's face, as he knelt before the door, and did not dream that the panels and friezes she so much admired were the work of her lover's hand.

Hence it was but natural that the memory of him should grow more and more indistinct, while all the while Stuart Leslie was showing her the better side of his nature, and patiently and persistently trying to win her love.

And so it came about that she began to let her mother's suggestions have a place in her thoughts. She had a vague, undefined feeling, which she would have almost blushed to put into words, that she would have to marry somebody or spend her life alone. And if she must marry, Stuart would be less distasteful to her than most people.

It was not often such thoughts haunted her. Still, the seed was there and was sure to grow.

Then came the day of the funeral, and all Barwich turned out ; not so much to pay respect to the dead as to look upon the face of the living. For two whole days little else had been talked about, and Rex and his father had been lauded to the skies for their noble and generous conduct.

Mrs. May, as we have said, did not wish Evelyn to go. But the latter was firm. She had resolved to see Rex again, whatever might be the consequences. If he had really forgotten her and wished to be forgotten, she would see it in his look. But, oh ! she hoped he would recognise her. The very thought of his coming seemed to awaken all the fond memories that were beginning to sleep, and her heart ached all the day for the hour to come when she would stand face to face with the man whom she had loved so dearly in the past, and whom she could not help loving still.

'Well, Evelyn, if you will go,' said her mother, ' I will go with you. But I think you would be studying your own happiness by staying at home.'

'Perhaps so,' was the answer ; 'but I must go, nevertheless.'

Evelyn's heart almost stopped when Rex stood before her with uncovered head. He had greatly altered, was older and graver-looking, but handsomer than ever.

She waited with throbbing heart till he should raise his eyes, and when he did so she looked at him steadily, hoping and longing for a glance of recognition. But he might have been stone, or she the greatest stranger in the world. There was no glance of recognition in his eyes, no softening of his stern set lips. She would have gone to him before all the crowd if she had dared. She longed to hear him say 'Evelyn' once more in the old tone of tenderness. But clearly he did not want her.

If he had struck her she could hardly have felt it more. And yet she would not give up all hope. He might return to her when the crowd was gone. Surely he would not go back to London the same day he had come. The journey would be too exhausting.

'Would he come to Beechlawn,' she wondered, 'in the quiet eventide as he used to do?'

She could see the carriage-drive from where she sat by the open window. The evening was so still she would be able to hear his footfall if he came.

So she watched and waited. Lower and lower the sun sank in the western sky. The beeches burned and blazed in the yellow light. The distant landscape vanished in a golden haze. The rooks cawed and croaked in the far-off elms, while a faint breath of wind came up from the south, and shook tho poplars for a moment, then sighed itself away into silence.

Then a quick step sounded on the gravel, and Evelyn's heart leaped into her mouth.

'It is he,' she said, and grew pale to the lips.

The next moment the hot blood rushed in a torrent over her neck and face. It was not Rex, but Stuart Leslie.

'No, I cannot see him,' she said, rising to her feet and clenching her hands; 'and what is more, I will not.'

And putting on her hat, she stole quietly downstairs and went out at the side-door, hurried quickly across the lawn, and then made for the Thorbrig footpath. 'It was the path Rex loved, and perhaps old memories would lead him thither again.' Such was the thought that swept like a flash across her mind.

To speak with him once more, to have some explanation, even though they parted in anger, was better than this continued silence—better a thousand times.

So she hurried up the field and into the wood— all aglow now with light from the burning west. Through the long avenue she walked slowly to the very end, then turned and as slowly retraced her steps. When she reached the stile she sat down, and rested her face in her hand.

'My dream is ended,' she said with a sigh; 'now let me try to forget it. And yet how can I? He

14

has not the face of a deceiver. His treatment of
Jonas Brown shows him to be good and generous
still. And, oh, his coming has awakened again all
the love of my heart.'

The next moment she was startled by the sound
of a footstep near her, and, looking up, she found
herself face to face with Stuart Leslie.

'I thought you might be here,' he said apologeti-
cally; 'and so I came to look for you.'

'You should not have troubled yourself,' she
answered coldly; 'I am not likely to take any
harm.'

'Do not be angry, Evelyn,' he said humbly;
you must know how dearly I love you, and——'

'I am very sorry for you, Stuart—very sorry
indeed,' she interrupted; 'but——'

'Nay, there must be no more buts,' he said
quickly; 'I do not ask or even hope that you will
love me as you loved Rex. But after his scandalous
treatment of you to-day, I am sure you will never
think of him again.'

'I do not know that you are called upon to be
the judge of Rex Raynor's conduct,' she said
severely. 'Please let us drop the subject.'

'But surely, Evelyn, you have no further hope
or expectation in that direction?' he questioned.
'Excuse me speaking so plainly.'

She looked at him for a moment in silence, then
answered quite calmly:

'No, Stuart; I have neither hope nor expectation now. Rex is dead to mo, and I to him.'

'I am glad to hear you say so,' he said triumph-antly; 'I think he has acted like a villain.'

'Stuart!' she said, turning and facing him with flashing eyes; 'never say that in my hearing again; I know not what secrets underlie his silence. But it is not for you to judge him.'

'I cannot help it,' he said; 'when I see how he has made you suffer.'

'What I have suffered is my own affair,' she answered.

'Oh, Evelyn, you are severe,' he said, after a long pause. 'Will you not give me any hope at all?'

'I neither give you hope nor take it away,' she replied.

They had reached the lodge gates by this time, and Evelyn held out her hand to say good-night.

'Answer me one question,' he said impulsively. 'Have I as much ground for hope as anyone else?'

'Yes,' she said; 'and more.'

So they parted.

CHAPTER XXIV.

'A turn, and we stand in the heart of things ;
  The woods are round us, heaped and dim ;
From slab to slab how it slips and springs,
  The thread of water, single and slim,
Through the ravage some torrent brings !'
                                    R. Browning.

A MONTH later John and Rex had left London and were on their way to the sunny south. After that day at Barwich neither of them could settle steadily to work. The sight of the old home, the sweet country air, the quiet peacefulness of the hills and fields, the rich colour of moorland and forest, made them eager to get away from the dust and noise of the city, and the constant jostle of the crowded streets.

'We will join Sam Laerton,' John said to Rex a few days later; and if you don't mind we'll go a fortnight sooner than we intended.'

'I should be glad to go at once for that matter,' Rex answered, 'for in truth I am getting a bit tired of London.'

'Well, you know I resolved in the spring that I would not spend another winter in England,' John said; 'the fogs try me so terribly.'

'I know they do, father; and the sooner we can get away the better. There is no particular reason why we should stay here.'

'None at all,' John answered; 'we are no longer pinched for money, and a rest and change will do us both good. I think the sight of the old home has made you restless, Rex, just as it has me.'

'I really believe it has,' Rex answered with a laugh, as he bounded up the stairs to his own room.

But in truth it was not so much the sight of Barwich that had made him restless, as the sight of Evelyn. He had foolishly imagined that to look into her eyes once more would ease the pain in his heart; instead of which the opposite result had been produced.

He almost wished now he had not gone to Barwich at all. Evelyn's unresponsive look had spoiled everything. He and his father had talked about spending a few days there, and familiarizing themselves once more with old scenes and faces. But that one look at Evelyn settled him.

'Drive back to the station at once,' he whispered to his father; 'I will settle with the Vicar and cross by the fields.'

So his visit to Barwich had yielded him no ẹasure, nor pleasure to anyone else. Those who knew him in the years gone by talked of success having made him proud, and popularity having spoiled him. Poor old Dr. Moffat felt quite hurt that Rex had not called upon him, and thought it was too bad that when people became rich and successful they should forget their old friends. But as a set-off against this was the fact that he did not forget Jonas Brown; that his, in fact, was the only hand stretched out to befriend him in his poverty and disgrace.

For several weeks after the funeral, Rex and his father were frequently talked about at Barwich. The women said how handsome Rex had grown, and what a splendid face his father had; while everyone declared it was a noble thing to befriend Jonas Brown as they had done, and to give him such a splendid funeral.

If Rex had only stayed a few days at Barwich they would have made a hero of him; but they forgot the seeming slight after awhile, and even Dr. Moffat was ready to excuse him. Meanwhile amid new scenes Rex was recovering a little from his heartache and disappointment.

San Vera (the name will do as well as any other) at the time of which we write was only just becoming known to English people as a winter resort. It was not big and busy like Cannes and Mentone, or gay and artificial like Monto Carlo, nor seamy-looking and old-fashioned like San Remo. Yet it was as delightfully situated as any of those places. Fronting the Mediterranean, and surrounded on every other side by lofty hills, it enjoyed as mild a climate as anyone could desire. Oranges ripened on the trees at Christmas, and geraniums bloomed in March. Even the date-palm grew here and there in the open, and brought its fruit to perfection.

Already it had its little colony of English people, chiefly artists and authors, who met regularly to talk shop and discuss the latest English news. The artists liked the place because it was within easy reach of Genoa, and not more than a day's journey from Florence. The authors liked it because 'living' was cheap, no mean consideration with knights of the quill. While delicate people liked it because of the mildness of the climate.

Sam Laerton, an old friend of John Raynor's, had wintered at San Vera for several years, and it was on his recommendation that John and Rex resolved to spend a winter there. Neither had been abroad before, and so the beauty of the Riviera came as a surprise to them both. The lofty mountains clothed with verdure; the deep ravines and shaded dells; the rocky cliffs and headlands; the splendid carriage-way cut here and there through solid rock; the hard beach of yellow sand; and, above all, the lovely blue of the shining sea, made such a picture of loveliness as neither had expected to see.

Laerton had secured rooms which suited them

exactly, and in a few days both John and Rex felt quite at home, and were delighted with the change. Every day there were fresh arrivals at the big hotels which had been recently built; while gossip was abundant for those who cared for it.

Rex gave up painting, and took to botanizing instead. The hollow in which San Vera was situated narrowed backwards to a mere defile just broad enough for the river and the road. Half a mile up, this defile branched out into half a dozen other dells and ravines, all of them well wooded, all silent and lonely.

In his present mood nothing suited Rex better than rambling through these quiet glens. It was such a change from the constant roar of London streets, so restful after the busy life of the last few years, that he gathered strength and cheerfulness every day. Whether it was wise or safe to ramble so far from the town alone he did not stop to consider. Once or twice he had come across suspicious-looking characters, who might or might not be of the bandit class, but he scarcely gave them a second thought. He was like a schoolboy let out of school. He just gave himself up to enjoyment and thought of little or nothing else.

So matters went on for five or six weeks, and then Rex received something like a shock. He was looking carelessly down the list of new arrivals one afternoon, when he came across the names 'Mrs. and Miss May, Barwich, England.'

In a moment all the blood had left his face, and he sat staring at the paper as though transfixed.

'It must be them,' he muttered; 'but how strange!'

As a matter of fact, however, it was not strange at all, for they had wintered in San Vera for several years past, though Rex knew nothing of that.

The minutes sped on, and he still kept staring at the paper, though he no longer saw it. He was back again in Barwich, climbing the sunny slope of the field, or loitering through the dreamy wood with Evelyn leaning upon his arm. How accurately every scene had been photographed upon his memory! In the years that had intervened he had forgotten nothing. He had only to give himself up to the spell of the past, and it all came back again.

A street cry below the window brought him back to himself, and, getting up from his chair, he took two or three turns round the room.

'This is awkward,' he muttered to himself at length. 'I think father and I had better get away from here. If we stay we are certain to meet them. The places of public resort are so few that there will be no avoiding it. And I am sure it is best for me that I should never look upon her face again.'

Then he fell to musing on the fact that she was still Evelyn May. 'I cannot quite understand it,' he said to himself. 'If I live till the first of next May, six years will have elapsed since I left

Barwich. And if Stuart Leslie has not been able to win her in all that time, his chance does not look at all hopeful. She cannot care for him, that's certain. I wonder now——'

And once more there came into his eyes that far-away look which betokened that his thoughts were back again in the past. He had tried bravely to put Barwich and all its associations out of his memory and out of his heart, but without avail. One touch of kindred association and all the past lived before him again.

After awhile he put on his hat, and started for a ramble up the glen.

'I must fight the question out with myself,' he said; 'and I think I can fight best out of doors.'

The struggle lay between policy and inclination. Prudence urged him to get away from San Vera as quickly as possible. His heart urged him to stay. He liked the place; he and his father had comfortable rooms; several friends were near them whose company they valued; and last, but not least, he could not deny to himself that his heart was aching for just another glimpse of Evelyn May.

He walked at a rapid rate, for the December afternoon was already far advanced. Less than two miles away was a deep ravine, the solitude of which would suit his mood just now. Twenty minutes' sharp walking, and he turned suddenly round a large spur of rock and plunged into the lonely dell. The sides were rocky and precipitous, and its course tortuous and uneven. He intended to explore its whole length some day. He fancied from certain indications that there must be some caves at the far end.

Suddenly he was startled by a sharp cry which rang out a little ahead of him and echoed down the lonely dell. He paused for a moment, when the cry was repeated, but muffled this time and long-drawn. It sounded to him like a woman's cry for help.

Instantly he sprang forward at a rapid rate, and, turning a sharp corner, he came upon a scene that almost horrified him for a moment. A young and handsomely-dressed lady, with a handkerchief tied tightly over her mouth, was being dragged up the ravine, with threats of violence if she made a sound, by a brigand of the most villainous type.

' Hands off, you villain !' Rex shouted, as soon as he could speak.

And in a moment the fellow dropped the lady's hands, and, pulling a revolver out of his belt, fired at Rex. Before, however, he could pull the trigger a second time, Rex had sprung forward and dealt him a blow between the eyes with his fist, which felled him like an ox, the revolver at the same moment flying out of his hand. Instantly Rex rushed forward and picked up the weapon, and the fellow, seeing that his means of defence and offence were gone, sprang to his feet and bounded up the defile like a deer, and in a moment was out of sight. A shot from the revolver followed him, but without effect.

Then Rex turned to the young lady, and, pulling the bandage from her face, he stood for a moment as if rooted to the ground.

'Evelyn, you here!' he gasped.

'Oh, Rex,' was all she could say. And then she burst into tears.

He recovered himself instantly. 'There is not a moment to lose,' he said. 'The fellow's confederates may be upon us directly. Run on in front, and if I hear any of them following, I will turn and fire.'

She needed no second bidding, and in a few minutes they were out of the dark ravine and in the broader valley. Here she turned and looked back at him, and wondered at the look of suffering upon his handsome face.

'Don't lose a moment,' he said, speaking as bravely as he could; 'run your best, and I will follow as well as I can.'

She did not quite understand the purport of his words, but she ran on as he told her, till she discovered he was lagging far behind. Then she paused and waited for him, but wondered he should so reel and stagger while he ran.

'Don't wait for me,' he called in a feeble voice. 'Save yourself. I will run till I drop; but I shall never reach San Vera.'

Before he had finished the sentence, she had run back to meet him.

'Oh, Rex,' she exclaimed, her great eyes filling; 'you are not hurt, are you?'

'I am a little,' he gasped. 'I was too near for him to miss me quite.'

'Oh, Rex, why did you not say so before! Can I do nothing for you?'

'No, nothing,' he said resolutely. 'Don't wait. Get home as quickly as possible.'

'Nay, Rex, I will not leave you,' she said. 'You risked your life for me, and I am not a coward.'

He smiled feebly, while a look of admiration came into his eyes. He hungered to tell her of his love again, feeble and spent as he was.

'If you go, you may be able to send help,' he said, after a pause.

For a moment she stood irresolute, then rushed off like the wind. In half an hour she was back again, accompanied by eight or ten others, chiefly men. They found Rex lying by the roadside, near where she had left him, pale and unconscious, while his life's tide ebbed slowly away through a bullet-hole in his shoulder.

CHAPTER XXV.

'A moment after, and hands unseen
  Were hanging the night around us fast ;
But we knew that a bar was broken between
  Life and life : we were mixed at last,
In spite of the mortal screen.'   *R. Browning.*

A FORTNIGHT later the doctors had given up all
hope of Rex's recovery. In extracting the bullet
they had been very successful, and had quite
expected his speedy restoration, but unforeseen
complications had supervened. Instead of getting
better, he gradually grew worse, till now the end
seemed only a question of a few hours. Rex felt
himself what all along the doctors had feared, but
he made no sign. Life was still very sweet and
precious to him. But if it was inevitable that he
should lay it down he was not going to complain.
If the manner of his death had been left to his own
choice, he did not know that he would have chosen
differently. To have saved Evelyn from a fate that
was worse than death was worth living for and

worth dying for. She would think of him kindly now. Unwittingly he had atoned for that short month of deception, and when he was in his grave she would remember, perhaps, only what was best in his life, and forget all the rest.

One day, after the doctors had held a long consultation, he called his father to his bedside, and said, with a feeble attempt at a smile, 'And so they think I will not get better, do they ?'

'They regard your case as very serious,' John said evasively, and with a manful effort not to betray his emotion. 'But you know, Rex, while there's life there's hope.'

' Yes, I know,' he answered feebly; ' but I don't know that it matters much. I am not afraid, and I am glad I saved Evelyn.'

'She has called every day to inquire. I am sure it is a great trouble to her.'

' I should like to see her once more,' he said after a pause; ' I wonder if she would come.'

' I can ask her, at any rate,' John answered, and immediately left the room.

Ten minutes later, after a timid knock, the door opened, and Evelyn May came quietly into the room. She was very pale, and outwardly very calm. She had evidently braced herself for the interview. But the sight of Rex so pale and wasted broke her down completely, and with a low cry, ' Oh, Rex !' she sank upon the floor and hid her face in the bed-clothes.

She did not see the smile that lit up his face like a gleam of summer sunshine, but she felt his wasted hand rest timidly upon her sunny hair. For several seconds no words were spoken. Evelyn sobbed quietly, her face still hidden.

'The doctors say I will not get better, Evelyn,' he said at length; 'and so I sent for you. I thought I would like to look upon your face once more before I died.'

'Oh no; don't say that, Rex, don't!' she said with a great sob.

For a moment or two he stroked in silence her shining hair. It brought back to him memories of the past. He was back again at Beechlawn, and the world was full of love and beauty.

Then Evelyn raised her tear-stained face, and with a resolute light shining in her eyes, she said: 'You must not die, Rex. I shall never forgive myself if you do. I shall feel like a Cain upon the earth all the rest of my life.'

'To die for you, Evelyn,' he said with a smile, 'is not painful at all. It feels like an atonement for the wrong I did. Oh, Evelyn, you know not what I have suffered!'

'I have fancied you were glad to escape from an engagement that had grown distasteful to you, or you would have given me a chance to speak.'

'Oh, Evelyn,' he said a little bit reproachfully, 'I gave you time to write; and when a few months later it was reported you were engaged to Stuart

Leslie, I know then you had put me out of your life completely.'

'Engaged to Stuart Leslie?' she said starting up, with an indignant blush upon her cheek; 'and did you believe it, Rex?'

'What else could I do?' he answered feebly.

She did not reply; but she took his wasted hand in both hers, and for awhile silence fell between them. Then Rex spoke again:

'I have loved you always, Evelyn. And now, if you will tell me that you forgive me for any pain I have caused you, and that you will think of me kindly when I am gone, I can die content.'

'Oh, Rex, I have nothing to forgive,' she sobbed, lifting his wasted hand to her lips and kissing it. 'In your heart you have been always true; and could I have seen you then, these long years of silence need not have come between us.'

'But I deceived you,' he said, harking back to the old difficulty.

'Whether the son of Mr. Brown or Mr. Raynor, you were always Rex to me,' she said; 'and I have loved only you.'

For a moment he looked at her, with an expression of glad surprise in his eyes; while a smile, like a wave of light, swept over his countenance. Then he drew her face towards him, and their lips met in one long kiss of reconciliation and love.

The conversation that followed during the next half-hour we need not here repeat. Now that

15

the long-standing barrier between them had been broken down, they talked without restraint. Each had a thousand things to say to the other, a thousand questions to ask. And while they talked, holding each other's hand, how swiftly the moments flew by! Rex almost forgot his pain and weakness. In the bliss of those moments he seemed possessed of new strength and energy. Evelyn's radiant face and voice of music were better than all the medicines the doctors had prescribed. A new hope had come into his heart, and a new inspiration into his life.

When John at length came into the room he was surprised to find Evelyn still there. She came to meet him with a smile and a blush.

'I am Rex's affianced wife,' she said, 'and I am going to nurse him till he gets better.'

'Till he gets better?' John questioned, with a sigh.

'Yes, till he gets better,' she said brightly. 'I am sure he is not going to die. He is going to get well again for my sake.'

'God grant he may,' John answered fervently; but when a few minutes later he noticed Rex's utter exhaustion, he had no hope that Evelyn's prediction would come true.

During the night the poor fellow became delirious, and talked pitifully and sometimes incoherently about a beautiful star that had gone out in darkness; how the star might have been his, but he had not courage to climb the dark stairs of night to reach it. Then he would call for Evelyn to come back to him, to listen to his pleadings once more. Through long years of suffering, he said, he had atoned for those few weeks of deception. Would she be pitiful and forgive?

Evelyn, who sat by his side, listened with tearful eyes and an agony of suffering upon her face. His ravings revealed the depth and strength of his affection, and showed her how true his heart had been. But the revelation, to all appearance, had come too late. As the long hours of that solemn night wore on she gave up hope. She had found Rex again only to lose him.

During all the years of their long separation she had clung to the hope that God would bring them together again.

And now they had met in a foreign land. God had sent him to rescue her from a fate, the very thought of which filled her with horror. But in rescuing her he had given his own life. Here in the dim lamplight, in the hushed and solemn night, he was slowly dying. Here in a strange land, far from home and kindred, he would sleep. And she would carry back to England a breaking heart, and one sad sweet memory that would never die.

She did her best to keep back her tears, but they came in spite of herself, and rolled silently down her cheeks. As the night wore on he ceased to rave, and only moaned softly now and then

Evelyn, bending lovingly over him, thought the struggle was nearly over. Now and then she moistened his parched lips, and pressed burning kisses upon his broad, pale brow. But he did not heed her. He was wandering in a realm unknown to her.

At length she crossed over to where John Raynor stood, and laid her fair head upon his shoulder. ' I can bear it no longer,' she sobbed, and burst into a tempest of tears.

In a moment John's heart went out to this gentle maiden, whom he had scarcely seen until to-day. ' My child,' he said. ' God will help us.'

' But it's terribly hard for me,' she moaned ; ' for I have caused it all.'

' Could he have had his will, he would not have chosen differently,' John said.

' He was ever noble,' she sobbed.

' Yes, yes. A better son never breathed. And know, child, he is my all. All the rest have been taken from me ; they are sleeping far away, yonder in Aberfae ; and it comes hard in my old age to be left alone.'

' I will never leave you,' she said with a fresh rush of tears to her eyes. ' I will be as a daughter to you.'

And for answer he bent down and kissed her white, smooth brow, not once, but many times.

In the very early morning the doctor called again, and found him quietly breathing. Not even a moan escaped his lips now. Whether or not he was passing into the deeper sleep of death it was hard to say.

'He has reached the turning-point,' the doctor said. 'An hour or two at most will decide his fate.'

So they watched and waited as the slow minutes travelled on. By-and-by the pale, gray dawn began to peep through the shutters, and the birds to awake from their sleep; and still Rex slept on without a movement and without a moan. The doctor watched him intently, keeping his finger all the while upon his wrist. Near the doctor sat John and Evelyn, pale and silent.

And still the hand of the clock travelled slowly round the dial, and the day broadened and brightened, drawing out all the shadows, and filling the room with a rich, warm light. At length there was a movement, followed by a low moan; then Rex stretched himself feebly and opened his eyes, and looked around him. The next moment a faint smile of recognition stole over his pale and wasted face.

'There's hope now,' the doctor whispered, and proceeded at once to administer some stimulant. In a few minutes Rex was fast asleep again.

From that time the tide, which had ebbed so far, began to flow back again. Slowly at first, it is true; so slowly, indeed, as to be almost imperceptible. But after a few days it began to come in with a rush. The rapidity of Rex's recovery was a surprise to everybody. But then everybody did not know that a new hope had come into his heart and a new inspiration into his life.

A month later he was able to take short walks, leaning on Evelyn's arm. In March the weather was lovely, and he was able to stroll down to the sea and sit in the sunshine, and listen to the dreamy plash of the waves, and watch the light shimmering across the lovely waters. These were hours of unbroken peace and unalloyed delight. All over the past, he and Evelyn wandered again, recounting every scene and every struggle, every sorrow and every joy.

'We are none the worse, Rex, perhaps, for having wandered so long in the wilderness,' Evelyn said to him one day as they sat on the cliffs looking out over the shining sea.

'Perhaps not,' he said with a laugh; 'but it is a great comfort to have got into Canaan, nevertheless.'

'Isn't it beautiful here,' she said after a pause.

'Yes, I should regret the days going by so rapidly, only that the first of May is coming.'

'Oh, you foolish boy,' she answered, putting her white hand upon his mouth.

'I went away on the first of May six years ago,' he said. 'We'll honour the anniversary, Evelyn.'

'As you will, Rex,' she answered, a glad smile upon her face.

And so it came about that on the first of May

they were married. All Barwich turned out to witness the ceremony. Old Dr. Moffat seemed to have got young again for the occasion, and Rex's 'young men' of other years had a holiday in order to be present.

'She needn't have wanted her boy to be Jonas Brown's son,' a woman whispered in the crowd. 'John Raynor is a father to be proud of.'

'Ah, they were poor then,' somebody whispered. 'Ay, an' they kept poor till right was done,' the woman replied. 'But here they come. Ain't they a handsome couple?'

'Ay, she's the bonniest girl in Cheshire,' an old woman answered, who had come over from Thorbrig to witness the ceremony.

'An' he's as handsome as she is,' somebody else replied.

'Handsome is as handsome does, I say,' grunted a little man who was edging his way through the crowd.

'Then if that be so they can't be beat,' was the reply from several voices at once. 'They've done handsome, both of 'em.' Then the crowd divided, to let Rex and his bride pass through.

*   *   *   *   *

To the foregoing narrative we have only a few words to add. Mrs. Jonas Brown has got married again. As an angler for husbands few women have been more successful, but her daughters, Joyce and Julia, are still waiting for an offer.

John Raynor—in what he calls his old age— declares he is a happy man. He spends every winter in San Vera. But when in England, he seems most content when near Rex and Evelyn. Mrs. May still calls Beechlawn her home. But it hardly seems like home to her unless Rex and Evelyn are there. Every summer they come over for a month or two, and bring the children with them. And in the winter Mrs. May visits them in London, or goes with them to the sunny south.

Of Rex's fame as an artist I need not speak. His praise is on the lips of everyone who makes any pretensions to a knowledge of art. His pictures are in ever-increasing demand. But success has not spoiled him: Fame has not made him proud. He is the Rex of old; not perfect by any means, but a good man and true, for all that; full of kindly impulses, and ever ready to do a generous deed.

THE END.

BILLING AND SONS, LTD., PRINTERS, GUILDFORD.

www.ingramcontent.com/pod-product-compliance
Lightning Source LLC
Chambersburg PA
CBHW030358270326
41926CB00009B/1172